Energizing
STAFF DEVELOPMENT
Using FILM CLIPS

Energizing
STAFF DEVELOPMENT
Using FILM CLIPS

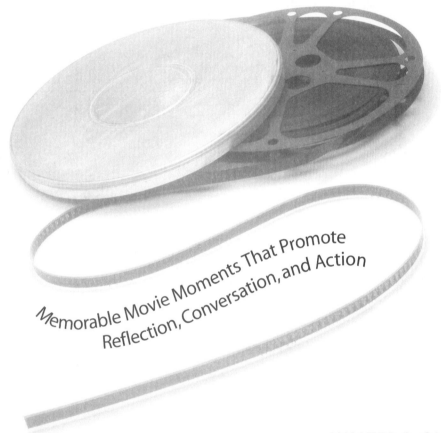

Memorable Movie Moments That Promote
Reflection, Conversation, and Action

WALTER R. OLSEN
WILLIAM A. SOMMERS

CORWIN PRESS
A SAGE Publications Company
Thousand Oaks, California

For information:

Corwin Press
A Sage Publications Company
2455 Teller Road
Thousand Oaks, California 91320
www.corwinpress.com

Sage Publications Ltd.
1 Oliver's Yard
55 City Road
London EC1Y 1SP
United Kingdom

Sage Publications India Pvt. Ltd.
B-42, Panchsheel Enclave
Post Box 4109
New Delhi 110 017 India

Printed in the United States of America.

Library of Congress Cataloging-in-Publication Data

Olsen, Walter R.
Energizing staff development using film clips: Memorable movie moments that promote reflection, conversation, and action / Walter R. Olsen, William A. Sommers.
    p. cm.
Includes bibliographical references and index.
ISBN 1-4129-1352-7 (cloth: alk. paper)—ISBN 1-4129-1353-5 (pbk.: alk. paper)
    1. Employees—Training of. 2. Motion pictures in education.
I. Sommers, William A. II. Title.
HF5549.5.T7O444 2006
658.3′124—dc22   2005008043

This book is printed on acid-free paper.

    06   07   08   09   10   9   8   7   6   5   4   3   2

Acquisitions Editor:	Rachel Livsey
Editorial Assistant:	Phyllis Cappello
Production Editor:	Laureen Shea
Typesetter:	C&M Digitals (P) Ltd.
Proofreader:	Kristin Bergstad
Indexer:	Pamela Van Huss
Cover Designer:	Michael Dubowe
Graphic Designer:	Scott Van Atta

Contents

Introduction

The Convergence and Conservation of Energy

A perfect storm is brewing in education, a convergence of forces that will yield powerful results in the near future. Just as the wave of computer and other technological advances has geometrically increased our ability to create, manage, and transmit information—which leads to increased productivity and job effectiveness—the forces at work now in education will ultimately transform the educational landscape.

Confronted with the sea change we are experiencing everywhere in our work lives, we find the idea of learning organizations compelling and believe that schools can and should be learning organizations. After all, learning is our product! Developed in the 1990s by Peter Senge with contributions from many people, learning organizations aim to harness the individual and collective capacities of the organization to leverage quantum improvement in personal and work efficacy. Developing a learning organization is complex, difficult work. The payoffs for success are potentially enormous for students, families, staff, and the larger society.

The energetic idea of the gathering perfect storm is a refinement and application of the idea of learning organizations in the field of education. None of us learn only by ourselves. Years ago, Lev Vygotsky said all learning is social. We learn with and through other people. Businesses want employees who can work with a diverse group to generate solutions to problems. Shirley Hord (1997) and others, like Rick DuFour (2004), have taken on the task of delineating learning communities in education. What emerges from this work is for schools to:

- Build an efficacious culture of collaboration and support based on articulated and shared values and visions
- Decrease isolation among staff
- Increase the frequency of focused conversations
- Develop more professional knowledge creation and exchange

A goal of our book is to contribute to the creation of reflective, conversational learning by individuals and organizations by providing opportunities for people to think and talk about important matters. You simply cannot have learning organizations without people who are conversing, thinking, and learning about their work constantly and forever.

Central to the development of learning communities is conversation. Some time ago, in an article in the *Harvard Business Review* (January–February 1993), "What's So New About the New Economy," Allan Webber asserted that conversations are what are new. He said clearly, "The chief management tool that makes learning happen is conversation." He also said that one of the manager's jobs in this new economy is to "facilitate the working conversations that create new knowledge."

In *King Arthur's Round Table,* David Perkins (2003) explores how we can make the conversations at the "round table" more intelligent and purposeful. He sees a smarter "round table"—versus the linear, hierarchical structures— as essential to higher functioning, more productive organizations.

Conversations are critical to facilitating learning at work and developing new knowledge. We hope it is apparent to all who read this that we desperately need to initiate quality conversations about the heart, soul, and mechanics of educating people in our schools as well as the infrastructure of the organization to support that mission.

We have found two protocols that are important to facilitating conversations. We are indebted to our colleague, Ron Petrich, an assistant professor at Augsburg College in Minneapolis and a member of our Red Pepper Learning Group, for introducing us to the idea of "third things." Ron brought the idea to our learning group because he explored the idea with Parker Palmer's program, "The Courage to Teach." Ron found the idea eminently useful in his teaching and training.

As we understand it, "third things" are texts, stories, poems, music, art, and songs that are brought into a learning group as a third voice that is different from that of the teacher/trainer or students. According to Palmer, "third things" are a connection to a larger world and serve the purpose of surfacing issues we generally would rather not deal with. According to Palmer, "You can't run headlong at deep questions." We see these "third things" as entry points into dialogue where we learn from and about one another. Above all, "third things" provide invitations to interact with other members of the learning community around very important matters. Goethe said, "Things that matter most should never be at the mercy of things that matter least." We think that dialogues of this sort help articulate our deepest values and most cherished beliefs. "Third things" provide a common experience to explore and to react to, enabling discussion regardless of the kind of day that we have had. "Third things" are touchstones to help us think about our own unique situation using our imagination (see http://www.trininst.org/past/2002/palmer2.html for a speech in which Palmer explains his program). With this book we see the possibility of adding to the bank of "third things": stimulating, instructive, and thought-provoking film clips.

The second protocol related to dialogue is the concept of study circles. Study circles go by other names, for example, discussion groups and study groups, and we are sure there are others. Study circles are a democratic idea—everyone in the circle is equal and is encouraged and invited to speak his or her mind. We are peers exploring ideas and our reactions to them. Most often, there is a piece to read prior to the meeting/session: a report, an article, a chapter from a book. The idea is to discuss the material, explore implications, articulate possibilities, and test assumptions. As there is no decision to make, the purpose is not to debate or discuss; it is to dialogue, to understand, and to explore rather than to defend positions and ideas. The purpose of dialogue is to create knowledge and insight by considering and exploring ideas together. The process of dialogue is to actively listen, set aside assumptions, and focus on inquiry. The objective is not to stake out a position and defend it, but to work at understanding others' views and your own views more fully and more deeply, even while holding your disagreements and opinions in abeyance. It is a process that can help us to identify and articulate values we have, find areas of commonality, and engage each other so that we are no longer "working strangers." Dialogue helps to generate creative new insights into recurring challenges and patterns. It is an important process in the building of a learning community.

So, film clips give us an opportunity to explore our values and ideas, learn about one another, and, in the process, build a stronger learning community.

WHY THIS BOOK ■

We think that as many issues converge, more will be demanded of educators. A primary goal in writing this book is to save teachers, administrators, professional development specialists, and all leaders time. Time is the thing we all want more of and cannot, under any circumstances, manufacture. The only control we have is over how we use the time we have.

Time is a precious commodity for educators and trainers. Time may be the most precious nonrenewable resource that we have. In our "get it done" world, lack of time is a central problem for educators and trainers alike— people need time to explore, conceptualize, and organize resources for an effective educational/training experience. Judy Arin-Krupp said, "Adults don't learn from experience, they learn from processing their experience."

Primarily, we want to provide a resource for busy staff members. We also want them to be able to lead conversations with their staffs that will generate possibilities rather than keep a negative malaise in place. We intend that the clips we have organized will save you time, help increase reflection, and lead to thinking about more possibilities for solutions.

We think of our work as simplifying your job, saving you time, and making it easier to include stimulating, reflective, and energizing applications in your practice. By using this book you can easily access valuable resources that are commonly available but have not been organized until now. In addition, you access this clip resource at any time you choose. We organized the clips by theme, telling you where to start and stop the film.

We also give you some background about the film and the clip, as well as guiding questions to help stimulate discussion following the viewing. We also provide books, articles, quotes, and places to do more in-depth research or to follow up with study circles. Finally, we give you our thoughts about why we really like the clip.

We *also* have a desire to make the education of adults more interesting, relevant, engaging, and active. Clipped movie scenes enable all to participate in a dialogue based on the immediate and common experience of viewing the clip. Film clips also have the capacity to create icons in communities of learning by generating common reference points of experience to fall back on at critical junctures of development. (Think of the movie *Cool Hand Luke* and the "failure to communicate"!) Education and training are significantly more fun, interesting, and pertinent with this powerful technology commonly available. Movies are an opportunity and a resource too rich to pass up during trainings, meetings, reflections, and conversations.

Finally, R. D. Liang, the iconoclastic British psychiatrist, captures the breathtaking pace of change when he says, "We live in a moment of history where change is so speeded up that we begin to see the present only when it is already disappearing." We see this book as being useful to leaders and organizations in this time of incredible change to promote and provoke conversation about our most important matters. Given the importance of leaders and the critically important task of disturbing the system by leveraging conversations, we wished to create a hand reference with which you may do so. Whether it is a team meeting, a faculty meeting, or a training program, there is a clip in here that you can use to generate a different kind of conversation in your organization, one based on authentic and straight talk. And we bet you have some of your own favorite and pertinent clips that you would like to include in your practice as well.

■ THE FILM CLIP ADVANTAGE

High Interest

Clips are capsule-like stories that lend themselves to analysis because they so often feature situations and people that we can relate to. The stories presented in movies are modern-day equivalents of tales told around the ancient campfires or the classic stories of Aesop or Hans Christian Andersen. Movie scenes, when properly used, illustrate a theoretical principle in real-life situations, making it easier for the trainee or participant to see the principle in action. For example, watching the clip from *Driving Miss Daisy* reinforces the idea of the importance of self-control in conflict situations. Clearly the high standards and budgets of the film industry have created a rich resource of vignettes that we can use in training.

Film clips are visual and auditory and create emotional connections. Appealing to or stimulating multiple parts of the brain strengthens learning to a point that usually is not experienced in traditional settings. Therefore, we increase our ability to motivate and stimulate a more diverse set of learners.

Stories and characters from movies "live" in the culture. Adults easily make connections. Movies are a familiar, comfortable medium in our culture today, enjoying a wide cultural currency. Many find that the stories and characters portrayed have relevance to their own situations and lives. People all over have experience with favorite scenes. What are your favorite movie scenes? Why? Ask friends what favorite scenes they have and what draws them to those scenes, and you will invariably get spirited answers. And your friends will probably be able to tell you why those are favorite scenes—a lesson was taught, an emotion was stirred, or a value was reaffirmed.

Film clips are engrossing, colorful, and frequently appear with music that stimulates more attention. Some are humorous, adding to workshop energy. The scenes are powerful, vivid examples of life situations that are full of meaning. Clips invite participants to think, interpret, discuss, and explore different perspectives and opinions or realities. Film clips also can help students/participants think about alternative behaviors and approaches.

Film clips help to illustrate principles and/or illustrate behaviors being covered in the course or training session. They add "real-life" dimension to what sometimes is an abstract or distant theory.

Focus

A film clip increases visual impact to illustrate a point—clips sharpen focus. Watching a whole video reduces the focus and meaning for participants, because they get lost in the volume of information, stories, and situations that are not related to the main point being considered. On the other hand, with a short introductory setup and a short time from beginning to end, clips lend themselves to shorter, more concentrated experiences.

Convenience

Video recorders/players are commonly available in schools or at training sites. The portable DVD player now is also becoming more common and less expensive. Once cued up, film clips can be cabled through an LCD projector to a larger screen for clearer viewing in a larger facility with a larger group. Similarly, video players and portable DVD players can be cabled through regular TVs with smaller groups.

Videocassettes are available for loan in libraries. Cassettes are inexpensively priced at half-price or online bookstores, at closeouts in discount department stores like Target, at garage sales, and at pawn shops. Tapes and DVDs are conveniently available for rent at reasonable prices for extended periods of time from neighborhood video stores. Netflix (www .netflix.com) is an example of an online rental service that sends DVDs via mail directly to your mailbox, and you can keep as many as three discs for an unlimited time period.

While showing film clips right from the DVD player or the videocassette recorder yields great results, there is an extra, added bonus, if you choose to go farther with technology. Recent and continuing rapid advances in computer technology have made video available on the desktop computer as well. For example, with the advent of iMovie (and other computer programs for Macs and PCs) and converters (like Hollywood Dazzle) that take analog signals (videotape) and convert them to digital (computer), it is easy to import and edit individual scenes from a movie on the computer, turning the scenes into *QuickTime* files. Once in *QuickTime*, the files can be dropped into a *PowerPoint* or *Keynote* presentation, shown on a computer or television screen, or projected via an LCD projector to a larger screen. Check further with media specialists and user groups, or gather related information on the Web about capturing clips for use in your presentations.

As you have probably guessed by now, the ability to put the *QuickTime* files into a presentation enables a more interesting, complete, and integrated exploration of a topic or concept. You quite simply have more options and greater control over your presentation. By using slides before and after the clip, teachers and trainers are able to introduce and explain a concept. A central question can be posed on-screen to set up the clip. The follow-up questions for discussion or further instruction could take place after the viewing.

Film clips, whether delivered via computer or straight from the videocassette head to a TV or large screen, are powerful packages in the hands of teachers and trainers, enhancing our ability to deliver effective instruction.

Flexibility

You can use film clips at any juncture of your instruction—at the beginning to introduce a topic, in the middle to change the pace of the course, or at the end to reinforce your work. For example, you might use the *City Slickers* clip "One Thing" at the beginning of a training session or program where participants (such as a site-based management or leadership team) will be creating a mission statement or strategic plan. The clip helps to draw attention to figuring out what the "one thing" is in a unique and interesting, light-hearted way.

Or you might show the *Cider House Rules* clip "Power of Symbolism" during work you may be doing about school culture with school or district leaders—or conclude your work with the clip to reinforce what you have learned and talked about and planned for.

And because film clips are short experiences (most often fewer than five minutes) and easy to set up, the choice is yours about when to best use the clip.

Time

One reason to use film clips is that they are efficient—they save time. Training, meetings, and class times are usually packed with valuable activities, new knowledge, and collaborative work. Taking two hours from a tightly packed schedule to view an entire movie is normally impossible, yet we still want our participants to get the most learning possible.

A five-minute or less film clip is more efficient and convenient and focuses attention more narrowly than an entire movie. Clips can be cued up conveniently ahead of time to the exact spot needed. Time can be used productively after viewing for further dialogue and/or learning.

WHAT'S THE BIG IDEA? ■
HOW DID WE GET HERE?

For years we have seen gifted trainers and university teachers use film clips in exciting ways. Further, as we talked about it, we were able to identify and share several favorite scenes that we each had used—and where the scenes fit into our training designs.

Talking further, we also were able to identify other appropriate scenes that could be developed and included in our future training designs—if only we took the time to organize our thoughts using the rich resource pool that seemed available to us. These clips come from:

- Our own personal collection, which we have taken time to develop in our practice
- Other trainers we have observed and experienced
- Conversations with many others about their favorite clips and what the clips had to teach

We quickly concluded that the film clips seemed to fit many different purposes. There wasn't a common set of film clips used by all. It seemed like a disorganized yet copious source of training potential. There seemed to be an identifiable, rich, and varied pool of scenes to choose from that could match our training needs. Each clip made a powerful point. So we began to look for a reference where we could get more ideas for our own training. While there were a number of books (included in the Resources section at the end of each chapter) that dealt quite nicely with complete movies, we did not find many references of much use that pointed us to specific clips for use in the training that we do or university classes we teach.

We reached another exciting conclusion as well. While most people have favorite scenes from the movies and can articulate their thoughts and feelings about them, seeing the possibilities in clips for training is a new experience for most people. I (WO) remember when I first learned about systems thinking and experienced systems maps with loops and variables. Our friend and teacher, Michael Ayers, a Minneapolis consultant, told us that, after a while, we would be able to "hear" the systems at work in the stories we read or heard people tell. And he was right! The first time that happened to me, it was stunning. It became easier to see the systems at work. It is as if the new, special knowledge makes you sensitive to another dynamic of life that has been hidden until now.

So it is with film clips. Once you experience the unique capacity of film clips to provoke thought, once you reflect on their appropriate use, you will see films with a new set of glasses—your new frame will enable you to see every new scene as an exciting potential resource for your work.

■ DESIGN IDEAS FOR BUILDING AN EXCITING LESSON

You probably already have many lessons, lectures, and activities to engage students. Great! Find the topic and browse the film clips to choose an appropriate clip to include in your presentation/class. Give it a try. You may already be familiar with many of the movie scenes in this book or have your own favorites in mind that match your design needs.

Use a clip at the beginning to set up the theory or concept of the lesson or reading. For example, use the clip from *Cider House Rules* ("Power of Symbolism") to introduce participants to the importance of ritual and celebration in healthy cultures. Follow up the viewing of the film clip with a study circle lead by a team of participants on positive school cultures, using a cited article such as "Good Seeds Grow in Strong Cultures" (Saphier & King, 1985).

Use a film clip at the end to reinforce material and concepts that you have covered. For example, show the clip from *Driving Miss Daisy* about conflict and have the students identify the elements of dealing with conflict in a healthy manner. You could precede the showing of the clip with a study circle using one of the articles about conflict listed in the chapter.

Or use a film clip in the middle to prompt interest, change pace, and stimulate discussion. For example, the clip from *A Few Good Men* about handling the truth might be a welcome and thought-provoking break from the hard work you have been doing on some aspect of organizational development. Placed just right, it could reenergize the learning experience by giving the participants an opportunity to talk about how well they, in their organization, tell and handle the truth or other ethical dilemmas related to their work.

Film clips are very useful for examining parallel situations in the work environment, so make sure you take advantage by relating elements in the clip (characters, conflict, plot, outcome, impact, etc.) to the work environment. People are sometimes more comfortable about talking through sensitive and hard issues in a clip rather than talking directly to a person in the organization. Once connections are made it is easier to get people to talk about the real issues that exist in the workplace. A movie scene that presents a graceful act to diffuse conflict or deal skillfully with a difficult situation can be used to prompt discussion about our own actions in our environment. The key question becomes, Where in your environment, in your work life, can you benefit from what you have just viewed? How can you act more productively or authentically? In addition, what is standing in the way of your being more adaptive and skillful?

Film clips offer a chance for participants to catch their breath while engaging in a worthwhile, stimulating, and thoughtful activity. For example, you could show a group the clip from *Ice Age* and talk about the fable and how it relates to their work lives using the questions provided as a jumping-off point.

You could simply check the Contents for relevant topics or browse through the films in each chapter or topic, letting your mind wander through the descriptions and questions. See how we suggest using a film clip, why we really like it, or invent your own use. As you browse, you will likely begin to sense where particular scenes fit into your practice or training. It might even call to mind other scenes not included in the book that you see as possibilities. Be sure to use the space we have provided in the book to make notes about ideas that come to mind. Write them down right away! We are betting that you already have scenes that you would like to develop, so the book will give you an idea of how to organize your clips.

Despite the descriptions about the film and the scene, **it is important that you preview the clip before you use it**. Make sure you are clear about where and how you will use it. Look over the accompanying questions; add your own questions and quotes to leverage the power of the film clip.

We have also included a warning where language might be offensive. Many of the offensive words are now commonly heard on the radio or television, but we did want to call your attention to this because it may be a problem for you in your environment.

PLANTING AND NURTURING YOUR OWN ■ SEEDS: BUILDING YOUR OWN CLIPS FILES

Once you begin to use the medium, once you see the power you have to take lessons in new, productive directions, you will be excited by every movie you see, either brand new or old. You will have a new perspective from which to view movies with more insight and sensitivity. In this visually rich and diverse world, think about the abundant resources that are readily available. (*Leonard Maltin's Movie Guide* [2005] has more than 18,000 entries!) And we are only beginning to understand how to use them.

We are excited when we think of the virtual library that can be built of scenes that can be used for instruction. Technology has moved us to the point where we can collect film clips as we would other "third things" that we use in training: insightful poems, provocative stories, engaging exercises and games, humorous cartoons, and so on. While we have identified some film clips, we are confident that this is only a small beginning. We know that we can benefit from the work of others as they apply this rich resource to their work. Think how we can enrich our discussions, possibilities, and resources by trading ideas with one another!

Most of the teachers and trainers we know experience teaching as a way of life. It is always with us, and we are constantly looking for ideas, approaches, stories, and other material that we can use to better our craft— to make that one point clearer or crisper. And so we turn to films. Every film experience is a chance to find that one nugget you need to make your lesson the work of art that you always wanted to achieve.

■ WHAT YOU WILL FIND IN THE BOOK

We have divided the book into chapters that focus on training themes: conflict, courage, persistence, creativity, keeping hope alive, and change. All of the themes seem extraordinarily pertinent to adults in our schools and organizations today. You will find some of our thinking about the theme in the introductory section at the beginning of each chapter.

The "Clips" section of the chapter follows next. What we are attempting to do is to provide a template to use, not tell you exactly how to use the film. In other words, this is the way we see the clip being used, but it is only one way of many. We know that you will create your own best use for these clips. We also know that you will generate many more possibilities with many more clip ideas. The idea of this book is to make it easy for you to access a clip you may have already seen and want to include in your practice. We would like you to consider our approach to a scene just that: a place to start. You may have a different idea about or interpretation of the film clip, and that diversity of perspective is incredibly valuable. It is the same diversity of view that you will experience in the discussion of the scenes with participants after viewing.

With each clip you will find:

- Themes that the clip deals with
- The film title, year of release, and a synopsis of the film
- A clip summary; that is, what you will see in the clip
- The time you start the clip and the time you stop the clip. Start and stop times are given in hours, minutes, and seconds as tracked by the machine's real-time counter. Because many films may have various previews in front of the main feature, time is marked from roughly the middle of the studio's logo, usually just before the film starts. In other words, set the counter to zero when you see the studio's logo. Some studios start with a "home video" logo that is quickly followed by the studio logo. Times will not be "exact"as in "scientifically exact." Times may vary somewhat, but only by a little, probably not by more than five to ten seconds. For example, whether you watch a cassette or a DVD might lead to some time differential. It is just one of those inherent problems. To make it easier for you to cue up the starting point, we have provided a detailed description and/or dialogue about where to start and stop the clip.
- The approximate length of the clip given in minutes and seconds
- "Questions for Discussion"—which are starting points and are not meant to be limiting. Use the space provided in the book to add to this start.
- "Why We Really Like This Clip"—where we tell you why we chose the clip, what it illustrates to us, and/or what dilemma is featured. It is our commentary on the clip.
- "Notes" is a section for you to make notes in before and after you use the clip. USE IT! We think it is important for you to have room

to note your thinking with some room to write rather than simply make short notations in the margin. It has been our experience that, in the course of using the clips, adults invariably offer new interpretations and questions. Or you may be struck with additional insights or questions as you listen to or facilitate a dialogue.

"Field Work: How Does This Work in Real Time With Real People?" is the next section of the chapter. It is a "mini" training module. We focus on explaining how the clips, quotes, articles, or books work in an integrated fashion with each other. It will give you a sense of how the different activities flow with one another into a coherent whole. These are stories from the field based on our experiences.

The next section that you will find in the chapter is "In Other Words: Quotes for Extending Thinking and Conversations," which contains relevant quotations that you could use in your work. At times we use quotations to foreshadow conversations. You might post some quotations around the room and have the participants stand by the one that has meaning for them, talk with the group that shows up there, and report out to the larger group. Alternatively, you might use them in your presentation. Finally, you could use them to prompt further discussion about the issue, as in, "To what extent do you believe this statement? Why?" You get the idea. There are other ways in which quotes could be used as well.

We include in the next section, "Articles for Study Circles," a list of short articles that lend themselves to small-group dialogues, much like a book club would choose a book to read and examine together. Much has been written of late about the importance of conversations in healthy organizations. Whether they are called "study circles," "study groups," or "learning circles," they are a methods of building personal and organizational capacity by having peers consider information in articles or books through reading and discussion. An additional consequence is people getting to know each other, talking about values, and sharing and creating knowledge together, especially if the groups have been prepped with the concept and practices of dialogue (see *Whole-Faculty Study Groups: A Powerful Way to Change Schools and Enhance Learning* by Carlene U. Murphy and Dale W. Lick, and check for more information about developing study circles in your practice).

Each chapter concludes with a listing of books, "Books for Extended Learning, " that provide in-depth reading that deals with the theme. The list is not meant to be exhaustive or overwhelming. It is a short list, usually numbering less than ten sources, and the books are, in our view, the best we know of to explore the theme. A growing number of professionals are forming book groups as a way to increase learning and interaction, and these books could be handled in a similar manner.

A final word about the themes. While each chapter has a different theme and is presented alone, all of the themes are related. Life is not as neat. The lesson is that many of the clips can be used for more than one theme. To cite just one example, the clip from *Apollo 13*, "Conflict in Space," included in the chapter on conflict, might also be used to illustrate the courage of one's convictions or keeping hope alive by focusing on the task at hand. So having an open and flexible approach will yield more possibilities.

Enjoy!

■ RESOURCES

http://imdb.com/ is the URL for the Internet Movie Database. IMDB is a gem. We will not go into all of the features here, but you can use it to find vast amounts of information about a movie by entering the title in the search box. In addition, trailers are often available for viewing, and links to reviews are provided.

DuFour, R. (2004). What is a professional learning community? *Educational Leadership, 61*(8), 6–11.

Hord, S. (1997). Professional learning communities: What are they and why are they important? *Issues . . . About Change 6*(1) [available online at http://www.sedl.org/change/issues/issues61.html].

Maltin, L. (2005). *Leonard Maltin's movie guide* (2005 ed.). New York: Plume.

Murphy, C. U., & Lick, D. W. (1998). *Whole-faculty study groups: A powerful way to change schools and enhance learning.* Thousand Oaks, CA: Corwin.

Perkins, D. (2003). *King Arthur's round table.* Hoboken, NJ: John Wiley.

Saphier, J., & King, M. (1985). Good seeds grow in strong cultures. *Educational Leadership, 42*(6), 67–74.

Simon, S. (2002). *The force is with you: Mystical movie messages that inspire our lives.* Charlottesville, NC: Hampton Roads.

Solomon, G. (1995). *The motion picture prescription: Watch this movie and call me in the morning.* Santa Rosa, CA: Aslan.

Solomon, G. (2001). *Reel therapy: How movies inspire you to overcome life's problems.* New York: Lebhar-Friedman.

Teague, R. (2000). *Reel spirit: A guide to movies that inspire, explore and empower.* Unity Village, MO: Unity House.

Webber, A. (1993, January-February). What's so new about the new economy. *Harvard Business Review.* Boston: Harvard Business School Publishing.

Acknowledgments

This book represents our continual search for making impacts that lead to action for educators. We love stories, quotes, and film clips as training tools to increase understanding, reflection, and putting ideas into action. We have used film clips in our classes and training sessions; we have seen the power of these clips to create the environment for new thinking and, most of all, the conversations that create new applications. We are grateful to many people who have contributed to our success and our learning. We hope this book contributes to the ability of committed adults to have conversations of the highest order about things that really matter about the continuing education of our children and ourselves.

I ("Skip") want to acknowledge the contributions of many friends and colleagues who have talked with me about their favorite films and scenes. This collection simply would not have been possible without them.

Most of all, Bill, I admire your questions and your sense of humor, and I count myself lucky to be in your presence. This has been a real kick, writing this book with you, and I'm looking forward to all the projects that have been conceptualized and born in our conversations.

Finally, to my wife Janet, I am extraordinarily grateful for your warmth, creativity, intelligence, and support. Your counsel and wisdom in our conversations about movies and clips are woven throughout the book. Thank you.

I ("Bill") wish to acknowledge Suzanne Bailey, who was the first person I saw use film clips to inspire thinking. Her teaching and modeling have been paramount in shaping my professional development activities. I owe special thanks to Dr. Jennifer York-Barr for her work at the University of Minnesota and the Professional Development Leadership Program, and inspiring educators to be learners and professionals. I am grateful for our collaborative projects. Thanks are due to Terrence Deal, whom I have watched use video clips in his presentations. He provided many ideas on how to engage people and increase meaning. Thank you to Temple, my daughter, and Perry, my son, for introducing me to movies that I would have never seen and for expanding my thinking with your questions. Both of you are an inspiration to me. Skip, I continue to be energized and touched by our conversations, writing, and training projects, and look forward to many more projects in the future.

We both recognize Angeles Arrien and Patrick O'Neill, both of whom continue to expand our thinking and model the use of film clips in personal and professional learning. Thanks to Education Minnesota and the TALL (Teachers as Leaders and Learners) project for allowing us to work with teachers in the state of Minnesota and allowing us to experiment with the use of film clips. We are also very appreciative of the NSDC for the opportunity to present at national conferences and their total commitment to serving educators. The mission and vision of the NSDC inspires us to continue making a difference for all staff.

Finally, we appreciate Rachel Livsey at Corwin Press for supporting this project. After the NSDC conference in New Orleans, Rachel approached us about this possibility. Thank you for your encouragement and support for our work.

—Walter "Skip" Olsen
—William "Bill" Sommers

The contributions of the following reviewers are gratefully acknowledged:

David Hyerle
President
Designs for Thinking
Lyme, NH

Pam Robbins
Learning Consultant
Mt. Crawford, VA

Karen Hayes
Assistant Professor
Department of Educational Administration and Supervision
University of Nebraska Omaha
Omaha, NE

About the Authors

Walter R. "Skip" Olsen has been a social studies teacher and a high school guidance counselor and has served as a business agent for the Minneapolis Federation of Teachers. He was educated at Trenton State College in New Jersey and the University of St. Thomas in St. Paul, Minnesota. As an adjunct professor at the University of St. Thomas and St. Mary's University, he taught courses on leadership, management skills, organizational development, and educational reform. He taught use of the Internet for research at Open University. Skip has consulted with teachers unions, schools, and school districts. As a teacher and consultant Skip has used film clips, stories, poems, and music extensively to initiate and enhance dialogues. He resides happily in Minneapolis with his wife, Janet. Skip would love to hear from you about your practice related to using film clips, stories, poems, and music—his email address is wolsen@mn.rr.com.

William A. "Bill" Sommers of Edina, Minnesota, is currently the principal of Chaska High School in Chaska, Minnesota. He is also a Senior Fellow for the Urban Leadership Academy at the University of Minnesota. He is on the Board of Trustees and is President-elect for the National Staff Development Council. Bill is the former Executive Director for Secondary Curriculum and Professional Learning for Minneapolis Public Schools and is also an adjunct professor of educational leadership at Hamline University in St. Paul. Since 1990, he has been an associate trainer for the Center for Cognitive Coaching based in Denver, Colorado. Bill has co-authored four books, *Living on a Tightrope: A Survival Handbook for Principals, Becoming a Successful Principal: How to Ride the Wave of Change Without Drowning, Reflective Practice to Improve Schools*, and *A Trainer's Companion*. In addition to writing many articles regarding coaching, assessment, and reflective thinking, he also does training in poverty, leadership, organizational development, conflict management, brain research, and classroom management. From 1970 to the present he has been in K–12 education as a teacher and principal in urban and suburban schools. Bill also has served as an adjunct faculty member at the University of St. Thomas, St. Mary's University, Union Institute, and Capella University.

Film Clips That Explore Conflict

Conflict is the gadfly of thought. It stirs us to observation and memory. It instigates to invention. It shocks us out of sheep-like passivity, and sets us at noting and contriving.

—John Dewey

At the time of this writing, the world seems to be filled with a greater-than-usual amount of destructive conflict. Internationally, we are at war in Iraq and Afghanistan. Christians and Muslims are fighting in India. Arabs and Jews are killing one another by scores. Catholics and Protestants continue to be at odds in Ireland. And the list goes on.

At home the situation, while not as violent, is destructive nonetheless. Legislatures are tightly deadlocked with sharp lines drawn about issues of abortion, gay marriage, education standards and funding, and the very purpose and extent of government and taxes.

There is a lament in the voices of many adults when they talk about the demise of civility in our everyday lives. We've felt it ourselves. Recently, I (WO) was struck by an extended conversation on the *Lehrer News Hour*. Two theologians who disagreed with one another about the impact of religion on the political process both here and abroad spoke to the reporter. I was impressed by their ability to disagree, present points of view, and do so with a serious and mutual respect, without acrimony or animosity. Many of our conversations about important matters today are polarized, personalized, and laced with hostility. We believe that the presence of honest, straightforward, even passionate dialogue without hostility will contribute to the success of our organizations. Our schools and our organizations are living systems, and, although creative tension can be helpful, hostility is harmful to living systems.

We are reminded of the first verse of W. B. Yeats's poem, "The Second Coming" (1919):

Turning and turning in the widening gyre
The falcon cannot hear the falconer;
Things fall apart; the center cannot hold;
Mere anarchy is loosed upon the world,

The blood-dimmed tide is loosed, and everywhere
The ceremony of innocence is drowned;
The best lack all conviction, while the worst
Are full of passionate intensity.

Given the social climate, it is easy for the business of organizations to be hijacked by destructive conflict. There are, and always will be, competing ideas about how to get things done. There will always be diverse values about what should get done. And there will always be different styles about how to go about work. There will always be differences, and hence the possibility of destructive conflict. The adaptive and generative organizations will create places where multiple points of view are discussed, considered, and understood before actions are taken. These systems will be able to ride the waves of conflict without being overwhelmed and paralyzed by toxic conflict.

So, being aware of healthy attitudes and behaviors with respect to conflict is a step toward seizing the energy of the situation and channeling it to productive ends. In addition, observing and talking about specific positive behavior can in effect help set behavior norms for effective problem solving. Creative solutions for messy problems will come from conflicting views and the authentic conversations that lead to understanding. How we manage constructive conflict will determine the effectiveness of solutions and our emotional commitment to implementing those solutions.

Who knows? Perhaps we will be able to change the dysfunctional, hostile, and unproductive environments by practicing and spreading by example more civil and thoughtful behavior. The French have a proverb: "Children need models more than critics." Managing and resolving conflict can be an important model for our students, staff, and community.

We must not, in trying to think about how we can make a big difference, ignore the small daily differences we can make which, over time, add up to big differences that we often cannot foresee.

—Marian Wright Edelman

■ CLIPS

Clip: Conflict in Space

Themes: Dealing with conflict, avoiding unproductive conflict

Film Title & Synopsis: *Apollo 13* (1995). Astronauts Jim Lovell (Tom Hanks), Fred Haise (Bill Paxton), and Jack Swigert (Kevin Bacon) and a ground crew led by Ken Mattingly (Gary Sinise) and Gene Kranz (Ed Harris) struggle to save the crew on a crippled space ship that is 205,000

miles from earth, headed for the moon, in 1970. An explosion onboard cripples the mother ship. They must figure out a way to stay alive and return to earth with only the dwindling resources that they have onboard.

Clip Setup: When Houston orders the "tanks stirred," Jack Swigert throws the switch to complete the task. When he does so, things immediately go wrong—there is an explosion, and the astronauts struggle to gain control of the module to stop it from spinning uncontrollably. An unidentified gas is escaping into space. Tensions between Fred Haise and Jack Swigert boil over and threaten to be destructive. Watch to see how Jim Lovell deals with the explosive conflict situation. *Warning:* **This clip contains language that some may find offensive.**

Start Movie: 1:24:46 as Fred Haise says to Jim Lovell, "Listen, I've been going over some stuff and I'm a little worried about this cold affecting our battery efficiency."

Stop Movie: 1:27:01 as Jim Lovell says, "Yeah, Huston, this is Aquarius. Go ahead."

Approximate Length: 2:15

Questions for Discussion:

1. What were your thoughts as you watched the clip? How familiar was this situation?

2. What were the ingredients of the conflict?

3. Which ingredients were most and least understood?

4. What specific behaviors does Lovell use to ameliorate the situation? What impact do the behaviors have?

5. What are some conflicts we are having in our environment and what behaviors would improve the situation?

Why We Really Like This Clip: Conflict happens, even on your way to the moon. Two features of the clip stood out for us. One was the intuition that Jack Swigert had about Fred Haise's holding him responsible for the malfunction of the tanks and the explosion. We all have feelings (almost whispers) like that frequently and must find ways to handle them without submitting unwittingly to destructive conflict based on unchecked ideas. The lesson for us is that we need to develop in ourselves and others the capacity to hear the whispers early on, so that we can respond sooner and more appropriately by asking questions and declaring what our feelings are so we do not keep them all bottled up. Pattern recognition and developing appropriate responses are what move us from good to great.

A second feature that we really liked is Jim Lovell's insistence that they come back to the tasks at hand. He respectfully intervenes and brings them back to the task—"There are a thousand things that have to happen in order and we are on number 8!" This strategy helps stop negative behavior and redirects that energy. In addition, Lovell finally says firmly, "We are not going to do this. We're not going bouncing off the walls for ten minutes 'cause we're going to end up right back here with the same problem—try to figure out how to stay alive." His voice is calm, empathetic, and reassuring when he says, "Jack, stop kicking yourself in the ass." Being calm, being assertive, and focusing on the task are great ways to avoid destructive conflict.

Notes:

_____

_____

_____

_____

_____

_____

_____

Clip: A Chance to Dance

Themes: Values; handling frustration, confrontation, and conflict

Film Title & Synopsis: *Billy Elliot* **(2000).** Eleven-year-old Billy Elliot (Jamie Bell) rejects boxing lessons at the gym and quite accidentally discovers a love and talent for dance. He struggles with his father (Gary Lewis) and brother (Jamie Draven) (both of whom are involved in an ugly miners' strike), who ridicule Billy's love of dance.

Clip Setup: Billy has been hiding his passion for and practice of dance from his family. His very supportive teacher, Mrs. Wilkenson (Nicola Blackwell), shows up at Billy's home looking for an explanation for why Billy missed an audition she had arranged for him. Observe the different ways of dealing with anger and frustration and the impact of those ways on the participants and the situation. *Warning:* **This clip contains language that some may find offensive.**

Start Movie: 00:58:00 as Mrs. Wilkenson walks up the street looking for Billy's house. As she turns to walk back down the street toward her car, Billy, his father, and his brother walk up the street, passing her. She says, "Billy?"

Stop Movie: 1:03:47 as Billy runs down the snowy street toward his friend after his dance of frustration.

Approximate Length: 5:48

Questions for Discussion

1. What were your thoughts and reaction as you watched the clip?

2. What were the outcomes each character wanted from the situation?

3. The characters in the scene—the dad, the brother, Mrs. Wilkenson, and Billy—each have different ways of dealing with a frustrating situation. How would you describe each? How would you assess their effectiveness in dealing with frustration?

4. What assumptions did you see the characters make?

5. The situation deteriorates (or does it?). How might the individuals have acted more effectively to deal with the situation?

6. If you had been present, what would you have done?

7. Are there any similarities to how we deal with frustration in our workplace? What can we learn from how these individuals dealt with the situation and with their frustration?

8. If you were drawing up a set of rules to manage conflict, what would some of them be? Explain why.

Why We Really Like This Clip: We found it so refreshing that Billy handled his anger and frustration by pouring his energy into dance and not defending himself or turning to angry recriminations. Channeling energy positively in a conflict significantly increases the chances of a constructive outcome. Juxtaposed were the boisterous argument that Mrs. Wilkenson and Billy's brother were having—a really smashing row. Clearly there was a conflict of values and assumptions related to dance, dancers, and people of the middle class. In addition, there was the frustration that Billy's brother was feeling about the strike at the mine, an outside issue that he clearly brought with him to the situation. The clip is illustrative of how complicated conflict can be. Often we fail to see the complexity (the other factors) and respond narrowly and incompletely.

Notes:

_____

_____

_____

_____

_____

_____

_____

_____

Clip: Dealing With Conflict

Themes: Conflict management, dealing with difficult people, positive mental attitude, flexibility

Film Title & Synopsis: *Driving Miss Daisy* **(1989).** A proud, self-sufficient, and aging widow accidentally backs her car out of her garage into a ravine. Though she is not seriously hurt, it scares her son, Boolie Werthern (Dan Aykroyd), into hiring a driver for her. The film documents the 20-year warm yet contentious relationship between Miss Daisy Werthern (Jessica Tandy) and Hoke Colburn (Morgan Freeman). Best Picture of 1989.

Clip Setup: You will see a series of incidents involving Hoke, a house-keeper named Idella (Esther Rolle), and Miss Daisy. Hoke's attitude and behavior finally yield success.

Start Movie: 00:16:34 as Hoke is dusting the light bulbs, Miss Daisy enters the room and says, "Here, what do you think you're doing?"

Stop Movie: 00:22:08 as Hoke drives Miss Daisy to the store, he says, "I just love the smell of a new car, don't you, Miss Daisy?"

Approximate Length: 5:34

Questions for Discussion:

1. What were your observations and reactions as the clip unfolded?

2. How would you describe Hoke's attitude and behavior?

3. What exactly did Hoke do that was helpful in the situations you observed?

4. What can we learn from Hoke?

5. How might what we learn from Hoke be applied to our own work environment? Where exactly?

6. How do we, in this environment, remain cognizant of these attitudes and behaviors? What steps can we take to promote healthier attitudes and behaviors in our workplace?

Why We Really Like This Clip: While the racist social conditions that Hoke and millions of other black Americans faced were deplorable and broke many a human spirit, Hoke was masterful in avoiding destructive conflict with Miss Daisy and remained an optimistic and admirable character. He might have succumbed at any moment in the dehumanizing and frustrating situation. Yet he chose to keep his eye on the goal of being of service to Miss Daisy as arranged by her son. And, although not portrayed in this clip, Hoke was not one to shrink from voicing his opinion. It is just that he chose strategically and well, always keeping a sense of a higher human value. Mulling things over, not taking the bait, staying in control of oneself, keeping focus on the goal—all of these are hallmarks of a master who avoids destructive conflict.

Notes:

_____

_____

_____

_____

_____

_____

_____

_____

Clip: Leadership: Introduction of a Plan

Themes: Leadership, dealing with divergent ideas

Film Title & Synopsis: *Flight of the Phoenix* (1965). A plane with oil workers and piloted by Frank Towns (James Stewart) is headed home. It crashes in a sandstorm in the Sahara Desert. The situation is hopeless—men are injured or have died, there are fights among the men, water is scarce, it is too far to walk out, there is excruciating heat in the day and shivering cold at night, and rescue is unlikely because the plane was way off course due to instrument malfunction. One of the dozen or so men onboard who survives the crash is Heinrich Dorfmann (Hardy Krüger), an airplane designer who calculates that it would be possible to use the undamaged wing of the downed plane to construct another airplane to fly them out of the desert. The film is about their struggle to work together to complete the task.

Clip Setup: Dorfmann excitedly reveals his analysis of the aircraft remnants to Captain Towns and Lew Moran (Richard Attenborough), the plane's navigator. He concludes that there are enough materials from the wreck to build another aircraft to fly out of the desert. The pilot and leader of the group, Frank Towns, reacts in a sarcastic and belittling way. Is it Towns's attitude, the plan, or Dorfmann's approach? Watch how a new, different idea is treated.

Start Movie: 00:36:41 as Heinrich Dorfmann, getting up from his chair in the shade of the aircraft wing, says to Captain Frank Towns and the navigator, Lew Moran, "Gentlemen, I've been examining this aeroplane."

Stop Movie: 00:37:38 as, after the exchange with Towns, Dorfmann walks up a sand dune to have a think.

Approximate Length: 1:00

Questions for Discussion:

1. How did you react as the scene progressed?

2. What is the impact of Dorfmann's idea on Towns?

3. What is Dorfmann's response?

4. What conclusions would you draw about new ideas and conflict?

5. What alternative behaviors could have been used by each man to create a better experience?

6. From watching the scene, what might we learn that may be applied in our work setting?

Why We Really Like This Clip: Fascinating, isn't it? Leaders are not always situated in the head position. Clearly Dorfmann was busy thinking about how to get out of the situation using the proprietary knowledge he had as an aircraft designer. Captain Towns, rather than being encouraging or asking how he could help, may well have foreclosed the only way the group had of getting out of the desert by not handling a new, deviant idea carefully or skillfully. A key question for us is, "How can we encourage divergent thinking without being threatened or hard-headedly sticking to what we think is the truth—the one right way to do it in the situation?" Beyond that, Dorfmann's response merits some examination about followership. What, for example, are the attributes of a great follower? How might he have reacted in a more productive way?

The clip challenges our ideas of the nature of leadership as well. It seems to us that the clip shows the dangers of one-person, positional leadership. The healthy, modern organization is more interested in developing distributed leadership across the organization, availing itself of everyone's gifts and talents, Dorfmann being the case in point. After all, leaders and followers do a dance that culminates in either success or failure, and here it was a matter of life or death.

Notes:

———————————————————————

———————————————————————

———————————————————————

———————————————————————

———————————————————————

———————————————————————

———————————————————————

Clip: The Park

Themes: Truth telling, kinds of knowledge, courage to recover from a setback

Film Title & Synopsis: *Good Will Hunting* (1997). Will Hunting (Matt Damon) is a naturally gifted math genius. It becomes apparent when he solves an arcane equation posted on a hallway white board by a famous MIT math professor, Gerald Lambeau (Stellan Skarsgård), as a challenge to his students. Will, working as a janitor at the school, solves the equation, to everyone's surprise. Professor Lambeau, seeing Will's gift for math, commits to helping Will turn his life from carousing with his buddy, Chuckie Sullivan (Ben Affleck), to more intellectual pursuits. Professor Lambeau finds Will's behavior and attitudes difficult and enlists the help of Sean Maguire (Robin Williams), a Boston psychologist whom Lambeau knew years ago in school.

Clip Setup: The first session in psychologist Sean Maguire's office with Will Hunting was a disaster. Will used his wits, verbal acuity, and cynicism to level Sean, keeping him off balance and at a distance. This clip is the start of the second session. Note how Will's quick mouth starts as soon as they sit on the park bench. Focus on how Sean deals with Will regarding his anger, frustration, and defeat. *Warning:* **This clip contains language that some may find offensive.**

Start Movie: 00:45:56 as Will is coming downstairs, going to Sean's office. Will opens the door, cigarette held in his lips, and says, "You again, huh?"

Stop Movie: 00:51:03 as Will sits alone on the park bench, looking at the lake.

Approximate Length: 5:06

Questions for Discussion:

1. What did you find interesting in the clip?

2. What is Sean saying to Will? How is he saying it? What do you find significant about the monologue Sean delivers to Will?

3. Given what you see, how would you judge the impact of Sean's confrontation?

4. To what extent were Sean's actions appropriate to the situation?

5. Another interesting aspect of Sean's talk is his drawing attention to different *kinds* of knowledge. He seems to imply that experience is at odds with "book" knowledge. How do you interpret the speech Sean gives with respect to the kinds of knowledge and how they are related?

6. Clearly Sean was taking a risk to move the situation along in a healthier direction. What risks should we consider taking in our work environment to move things along? Make them healthier?

7. What can we learn from the clip that we should keep in mind in our work environment?

Why We Really Like This Clip: We particularly like the courage that Sean finds to reflect on what happened during the first session, rather than avoiding the trouble. It reminds us of a proverb: The best way out is through. In other words, this is clearly a conflict situation that could have been ignored or minimized. Further, we admired the courage that Sean had to articulate his views forthrightly to Will, without blame or judgment, as our mentor Angeles Arrien (anthropologist, author, trainer) might say. Finding your voice is no easy matter. And, once you have found your voice—your conviction, your truth—it often takes courage to stand resolutely and to speak calmly. Finally, we agree wholeheartedly with Sean's ending, putting the responsibility for the future clearly where it belonged, on Will. Sean left the choice to Will, neither trying to coerce him to act nor to be a certain way, not investing himself in a particular outcome. Sean had room now to reflect and grow. So the lessons for us in this conflict involve deep reflection, courage to voice what you've found, and allowing room and respect for the other party in the conflict.

Notes:

_____

_____

_____

_____

_____

_____

_____

_____

Clip: Attitude Reflects Leadership

Themes: Leadership, team building, conflict

Film Title & Synopsis: *Remember the Titans* **(2000).** Based on true events, the story is set in Alexandria, Virginia, in 1971. Under court order to integrate the school system, a black high school and a white high school were merged into one school, T. C. Williams High School. Herman Boone (Denzel Washington), an outsider who is black, is hired as the new head football coach, displacing the previous coach, Bill Yoast (Will Patton), who is white, victorious, and popular. Yoast, who was a candidate for the head coach position, reluctantly agrees to stay on as the assistant coach. Now the team must be integrated. Of course everyone wants a winning football team. The story is about the ups and downs of relationships among the students and among the adults, as the town and team struggle with integration.

Clip Setup: Gerry Bertier (Ryan Hurst), leader of the white team members and captain of the team, and Julius Campbell (Wood Harris), leader of the black players, accidentally run into one another at the water fountain during practice. The conversation they have raises a number of issues.

Start Movie: 00:29:06 as #81 (Julius) stands up after drinking from the faucet. Gerry (#42) bumps into him and stops for a much-needed conversation.

Stop Movie: 00:30:44 as Julius says, "Attitude reflects leadership, Captain."

Approximate Length: 1:40

Questions for Discussion:

1. What did you see? How did you react?

2. How did each character deal with the conflict? How productive was the conversation? Why would you judge it so?

3. How true was Julius's statement, "Attitude reflects leadership?" How would you apply the statement to our work environment?

4. If you were a mediator in this conversation, what would you say is the common ground for the captains? In your opinion, did they discover a common ground? Why do you say this?

5. Both of the boys seem to be talking about the importance of being a team. To what extent are we a team in our work environment? Or is our culture one where, "I'm going to get mine"?

6. Does this scene raise any questions for you? What are they?

Why We Really Like This Clip: Things fester, like having a splinter. The skin becomes inflamed and sore and the discomfort ever more intrusive into your life, preoccupying your attention until you realize that the splinter requires some serious attention. That is a healthy first step—acknowledgment—followed by the necessity of facing the truth directly and taking action. That is what we really like about this clip: the suggestion that you must have courageous conversations about what matters most in order for things to improve. Most often, things will not improve on their own, automatically. People are called upon to act responsibly in order for change to occur and to create the desired environment.

The other remarkable and noteworthy feature of the clip is the authenticity of each of the players. There is nothing made up or specious. Everything is out in the open. They are behaving as their authentic selves, leaving no question about who they are and how they feel about the other person. So the second thing we really admire here is authenticity as it promotes clarity and connection, which are so important in resolving conflict productively.

Notes:

_____

_____

_____

_____

_____

_____

_____

Clip: Given Nothing for a Long Time

Themes: Values, empathy, conflict, problem solving, shape shifting

Film Title & Synopsis: *The War* **(1994).** Stephen Simmons (Kevin Costner) returns home from the Vietnam War to Mississippi in 1970. Although he is trying to recover his life (finding a job, dealing with posttraumatic stress), much of the film deals with his children's conflicts with other kids in the community who are bullies.

Clip Setup: It was a tough day at the county fair. Stephen Simmons's car will not start while he is in line to park, and he has an argument and a fight with the nasty father of the bullies his own kids have been fighting. Yet Stephen and his son, Stu (Elijah Wood), are in good spirits as they bid on a house that is for sale. To celebrate, they decide to get cotton candy for mother Lois Simmons (Mare Winningham) and Stu's sister, Lidia (Lexi Randall). Stephen tells his son to wait on a box where he is easy to see while he goes to buy the cotton candy.

Start Movie: 00:57:14 as Stephen Simmons asks Stu Simmons, "Do you want to kiss it for added luck?" as they drop an envelope containing their bid on a house into the box.

Stop Movie: 1:00:38 as Stephen Simmons says to his son, Stu, "'Cause it looks like they haven't been given nothing for a long time." Stu Simmons stares at his tormentors for a time, gets into the car after his father, and closes the car door.

Approximate Length: 3:24

Questions for Discussion:

1. What did you observe? What reactions did you have?

2. What lesson do you think Stephen was trying to teach Stu? Was it strictly a lesson or was it a value Stephen had?

3. When trying to characterize Stephen's gift of the cotton candy, we think of words like "gracious," "graceful," "extending," and "reaching out." What other words come to your mind? How are these words or concepts related to conflict? What can we learn here?

4. Where in our work environment do we have to be more gracious, graceful, open, and willing to reach out? Perhaps some of your words fit better than ours. What are the challenges to being more gracious, open, and so on?

5. How can we remind ourselves to be healthier about conflict? Are there any institutional protocols or practices that we need in order to create continuing awareness? What might they be?

6. An interesting group activity would be to look further at the song that begins playing in the background just after Stephen Simmons breaks up the fight between the youngsters. The song is "Follow" by Richie Havens, and it continues to play in the background for the rest of the clip. The lyrics are available all over the Web: (to "Google" it: lyric "richie havens" follow) or go to http://www .getyourlyrics.com/r/richie-havens/follow.html. The song is available for 99¢ at the Apple Store for download, or you may already

have one of the albums listed by the Apple Store when you searched for the song. We suggest you listen to the song with the lyrics in front of you and have the group participants underline any phrases that have a connection with the film clip. Follow up with a discussion about the significance of what the participants found.

Why We Really Like This Clip: We really admire the capacity Stephen Simmons had for doing the unexpected, thereby shaping the outcome more productively. We also admire his capacity to empathize with the kids who got the cotton candy. In addition, Stephen acknowledges his part in the situation by admitting to his son that he set a poor example for him by fighting earlier in the day. The ability to step back from conflict, see larger issues, empathize, see your contribution to the situation, and seize an opening by being creative and authentic can often aid in resolving a conflict more productively. What he did is nothing short of graceful; we should all be so creative, empathetic, and magnanimous.

Further, the clip provides an opportunity to talk about bullies (children and adults) and how to handle them. Children face them in school and adults sometimes face them in the work environment. Fear is frequently a by-product of the situation, and handling the situation is important. Here is a chance to think ahead about what is the most appropriate, productive thing(s) to do.

Notes:

_____

_____

_____

_____

_____

_____

_____

Clip: Each One Gets Five

Themes: Bureaucracy, beaten up on the job, psychosomatic illness, boss behavior

Film Title & Synopsis: *Joe Versus the Volcano* **(1990).** Joe Banks (Tom Hanks) is vaguely depressed by his life. He works in a windowless office with dull walls and fluorescent lighting, at a not-interesting job, and with people who are isolated and quiet. He goes to the doctor often, trying to find the source of his not feeling well. Finally, he is diagnosed as having a "brain cloud"—it is fatal, but he has a few more months of perfect health and the doctor advises him to live well in the time he has left. He quits his job and is approached by an eccentric businessman who makes a well-paying proposition that would send Joe to the South Pacific, where he could "live like a king and die like a man." Joe accepts and his journey to the island of Waponi Woo begins. The film involves an assortment of encounters with interesting characters before the completion of the deal: Joe has to jump into a volcano.

Clip Setup: Joe has not been feeling well, although he does not know what is wrong. In this scene, Joe is told by the secretary, Dede (Meg Ryan), that he needs to send each of his clients five catalogs. Joe says there are not enough catalogs to do that. The boss, Mr. Frank Waturi (Dan Hedaya), "handles" the situation, as we observe the conversation.

Start Movie: 00:07:28 as Dede sniffs, wipes her nose, and says, "Yeah, each one gets sent five catalogs."

Stop Movie: 00:11:11 as Joe Banks responds to Dede by saying, "I don't know," as he puts his eyes to the heels of his hands.

Approximate Length: 3:31

Questions for Discussion:

1. What did you find interesting in the clip? What were your reactions?

2. This is a somewhat complicated situation. What are the issues that are causing conflict in this scene?

3. If you were Joe, how would you have handled the situation? Further, how would you manage Mr. Waturi?

4. What conditions contribute to Joe's not feeling well?

5. In your own environment, are there similar conditions that make you uncomfortable or not feel well? Describe them and your reactions and feelings.

6. What might Joe have done to improve the situation? What are some things you could do to improve your own situation?

Why We Really Like This Clip: My goodness, what a work life! We really like the way the clip exaggerates the difficulties of Joe's environment and his boss, Mr. Waturi, and we really like the way we see so clearly how the difficulties affect Joe. We are afraid that this represents the work lives of many of us—while the details might be different, the experience, the feelings, and the effects are mostly familiar. The clip gives us an opportunity to think and talk (maybe even make a plan) about the kind of environment we want to create at work. It is about the importance of being proactive. There is an opportunity here as well to think about how to deal with a boss similar to Mr. Waturi. What can you do individually and collectively to survive that ignorant, abusive treatment?

The clip also raises essential questions about action: How long do we wait to take action that we know is healthy? What are the forces that keep us from acting? Do we have to wait for a debilitating diagnosis before we act? What kinds of supports are necessary to encourage people to act courageously?

We are reminded of Soviet author Boris Pasternak's quote, which fits here like a velvet glove: "The great majority of us are required to live a life of constant duplicity. Your health is bound to be affected if, day after day, you say the opposite of what you feel, if you grovel before what you dislike, and rejoice at what brings you nothing but misfortune. Our nervous system isn't just a fiction, it's part of our physical body, and our soul exists in space and is inside us, like teeth in our mouth. It can't be forever violated with impunity."

Notes:

_____

_____

_____

_____

_____

_____

_____

Clip: The First Meeting

Themes: Conflict, blaming, leadership and followership, civility, power, authority, accountability

Film Title & Synopsis: *Lean On Me* **(1989).** Based on a true story, Morgan Freeman plays Joe Clark, an outspoken teacher who is forceful, energetic, and critical (almost bitter) of unions and administrators who will not stand up and take a position. He might be considered arrogant, tyrannical, and even offensive in the positions he takes and the way he expresses himself—he is not submissive to authorities nor very sensitive to human feelings. He winds up as principal of Eastside High School in Paterson, New Jersey, when the superintendent of schools and mayor of the city need someone with a strong hand to turn the school around to avoid having the state take it over. It is the story of Joe Clark's attempts to turn a failing, drug-infested, dirty, unsafe, and undisciplined school into a place that is proud, disciplined, and successful.

Clip Setup: Joe Clark has been appointed principal of Eastside High School and charged with getting the place together to avoid a state takeover. We observe the first staff meeting with Mr. Clark as the new principal.

Start Movie: 00:13:47 as the new principal, Joe Clark, walks through the halls of his new assignment, where there is graffiti and trash all over.

Stop Movie: 00:17:37 as Joe Clark says, "Are there any questions?" Then he pauses and looks around. Clark finally says, "Mr. Wright" (Tony Todd). Clark then walks out the door with Mr. Wright, the head of security.

Approximate Length: 3:53

Questions for Discussion:

1. What did you see? What were your reactions?

2. How else might the first meeting have gone?

3. To what extent is conflict in this situation necessary?

4. What did you spot that exacerbated the situation? What did you see that was helpful?

5. Does Joe Clark have the authority to make demands? Explain. Does Joe Clark have the relationships in the staff to make changes? Explain.

6. What would you do if you were on the staff?

Why We Really Like This Clip: We really like this clip because of the strong emotions it stirs in us. It is illustrative of the old model of leadership, that is, the "new" leader marches in, takes "control," and "initiates" his new program to get results. While the model is appropriate in some circumstances, it is hard for us to see how this kind of beating people down can build a team, create energy, or get results. Joe Clark is clearly not aware that he cannot do this himself, that others need to be on the team. Besides considering conflict, the clip also allows us to talk about blame, leadership, followership, leadership style, abusive work circumstances, bullies, raising one's voice, and the best way to get results. The clip is rich in possibilities for discussion.

Notes:

_____

_____

_____

_____

_____

_____

_____

_____

Clip: Boone's Introduction

Themes: Conflict, self-control, leadership

Film Title & Synopsis: *Remember the Titans* **(2000).** Based on true events, the story is set in Alexandria, Virginia, in 1971. Under court order to integrate the school system, a black high school and a white high school are merged into one school, T. C. Williams High School. Herman Boone (Denzel Washington), an outsider who is black, is hired as the new football coach, displacing the previous coach, Bill Yoast (Will Patton), who is white, victorious, and popular. Yoast, who was a candidate for the head coach position, reluctantly agrees to stay on as the assistant coach. The football team must now be integrated. And everybody wants a winning football team.

Clip Setup: Tension is high in the town because of an apparent shooting and the forced integration of the high schools. Coach Yoast keeps his football players from participating in the trouble by rounding them up in his truck. Yoast brings some of the team back to the office, where Head Coach Herman Boone is waiting for his first meeting with Yoast.

Start Movie: 00:02:26 as a young man is running down steps toward the football team shouting, "They're coming down to the store!"

Stop Movie: 00:04:30 as Herman Boone says, "What an opportunity, then, for me to learn from the best."

Approximate Length: 2:05

Questions for Discussion:

1. What did you see? What were your reactions?

2. What are the sources of the conflict?

3. What alternatives might be developed for dealing with the difficulties in a healthier fashion?

4. What about Boone's behavior contributes to disarming the situation?

5. Consider situations in your environment where softness or humility might have been used to create more productive outcomes. Describe them and what actions would have changed the situation for the better.

Why We Really Like This Clip: Coach Boone is masterful at finding common ground, always bringing the conversation back to football, winning, and the reality of the situation. He keeps personal hard feelings out of it. He brilliantly disarms the potential conflict by saying, "What an opportunity for me, then, to learn from the best," recognizing and acknowledging the competence and skill of Coach Yoast. Yet Coach Boone manages to show his own competence by asserting, "I won a couple of titles down in North Carolina." So, finding common ground, appealing to the good senses of the potential adversary to recognize the reality of the situation, recognizing and authentically acknowledging a potential opponent's strengths while managing to state your values or strengths—all are great strategies for minimizing conflict and being more productive.

Notes:

_____

_____

_____

_____

_____

_____

_____

_____

Clip: Incomplete Conversation

Themes: Presumption, not listening, not questioning, conflict caused by incomplete information

Film Title & Synopsis: *Shrek* **(2001).** An animated film, it tells the story of Shrek (Mike Myers), an ugly, green, smelly ogre who lives peacefully by himself in a swamp. He likes his quiet life and is disturbed when the local Lord Farquaad (John Lithgow) evicts fairy-tale creatures from the kingdom and they settle in Shrek's swamp. Shrek goes to Lord Farquaad to complain. Farquaad says he will rectify the situation if Shrek brings him Princess Fiona (Cameron Diaz), whom he wants to marry. During the adventure to capture the princess and bring her to Farquaad, Shrek falls in love with her.

Clip Setup: Shrek has fallen in love with the princess and is approaching her cabin with flowers for her. He wants to talk to her and tell her of his feelings. As he approaches the door, he overhears a conversation between Princess Fiona and the donkey (Eddie Murphy), Shrek's friend. But because Shrek came to the conversation late, he has not heard what came before and does not know about Princess Fiona's secret transformation when the sun goes down and comes up; Shrek assumes the worst.

Start Movie: 1:03:24 as Shrek walks to a house, flowers in his hand, practicing what he will say to the princess.

Stop Movie: 1:07:20 as Lord Farquaad says to Princess Fiona, "You don't have to waste good manners on the Ogre. It's not like it has feelings." And Fiona replies, "No, you're right. It doesn't."

Approximate Length: 3:53

Questions for Discussion:

1. What did you see? What were your reactions?

2. What are things Shrek could have done to check his anger and subsequent behavior?

3. Thinking about your work environment, see if you can identify areas in the past when this dynamic played out. Describe them.

4. Again, thinking about your work environment, are there currently issues that could be straightened out with more information? Describe the situation and what plans need to be made to improve it.

Why We Really Like This Clip: This clip is illustrative of a common aspect of conflict: Everyone does not always have all the information. Assumptions abound. So it is clear to us that checking out assumptions is necessary to work our way through conflict. By asking if we all have the key information and going over it to make sure, we can take a step back from the intensity of the situation, which allows us to gather ourselves and look at something different. Doing so breaks the chain of events leading to unproductive conflict.

Notes:

_____

_____

_____

_____

_____

_____

_____

Clip: You Cannot See

Themes: Perspective, change, conflict

Film Title & Synopsis: *Teachers* **(1984).** Alex Jurel (Nick Nolte) is a teacher in a run-down high school. He has an easy, yet demanding way with students and is well liked by students though somewhat at odds with his colleagues. He speaks his mind and does not think the school is particularly good, and he is openly critical of teachers who are not doing their jobs. The school is being sued by a student who has graduated but still cannot read and write. The lawyer for the student is Lisa Hammond (JoBeth Williams), who is an attractive former student of Jurel's. Jurel and Hammond explore their relationship. The film is a snapshot of the school's diverse and interesting characters interacting with one another in comedic and dramatic scenes.

Clip Setup: Lisa Hammond, a lawyer representing a student who is suing the school because he graduated even though he cannot read or write, is at Alex Jurel's apartment for dinner, hoping to find out more information she might use in her case. Jurel is interested in her, and he is to testify at the trial. Hammond is Jurel's former student, he having been her favorite teacher. As the scene progresses, we see Hammond conclude that Jurel has become more cynical than when she was his student and is no longer interested in putting up "the good fight." *Warning:* **This clip contains language that some may find offensive.**

Start Movie: 00:57:34 as lawyer Lisa Hammond says to teacher Alex Jurel, "I can't understand the teachers," as she is cutting food and he is attempting to kiss her neck.

Stop Movie: 1:00:07 as Lisa Hammond says good-bye to Alex Jurel and walks down the stairs, leaving Jurel's apartment after the argument.

Approximate Length: 2:35

Questions for Discussion:

1. What did you see? What were your reactions?

2. Jurel says people make up "the system" but they do not want to be scapegoats for it. To what extent is that a plausible argument? To what extent is it an excuse?

3. Jural says everybody wants to change schools but no one wants to pay the price. To what extent is he right?

4. Zora Neale Hurston, in her novel *Their Eyes Were Watching God*, says "you gotta go there to know there." Jural raises the issue of whether people from the outside can see clearly or accurately what is going on in a school. He says people cannot see because they are hiding behind their memories and ideals. Are "outsiders" able to see what is going on in schools? Explain. Does being an educator in a school grant some kind of special knowledge or insight? Explain. To what extent do you agree with Hurston's idea of "going there to know there"?

5. What, in your opinion, is the conflict? Is this the "proper" way to proceed? What other ways might you suggest for healthier experiences?

Why We Really Like This Clip: The clip raises profound issues for the schoolhouse. The difference of opinions mirrors the dilemma for schools. When ideas, criticism, suggestions, and complaints come to school people, how should they be handled? What weight should you give to the feedback? And is it possible for school people so invested in their institution to sort out the information to get the nuggets that are germane? On the other hand, what damage is done to schools in the name of progress? Or what happens to a school when someone with an ax to grind continues to demand attention? How do we strike a balance? These are real and thorny issues for schools, especially in an era when there is no shortage of opinions about what should be done with and in schools.

Notes:

_____

_____

_____

_____

_____

_____

_____

_____

FIELD WORK: HOW DOES THIS WORK IN REAL TIME WITH REAL PEOPLE? THESE ARE THE TITANS ■

Diversity issues in schools can be volatile. Differences can also present a great teaching opportunity. For example, in two of the schools where we have worked, one in an urban setting and the other in a suburban setting, we had diversity clubs. The main purpose of these clubs was to promote understanding and provide a safe environment for people to find out about other cultures and share ideas. One of the schools and the local police department hosted an evening called "A Dialogue on Race," which was attended by teachers, parents, students, clergy, business leaders, and others from the community.

The event was held in the media center, so we were able to have people sitting at tables in groups of six to eight. As an opening activity, we printed a single quote about conflict on a one side of a piece of paper, so the quote took up the entire side. Each table had a different quote. The purpose of the activity was for all participants to introduce themselves to the group and indicate what had meaning for them in the quote as part of their introductions.

After reviewing the agenda for the evening, we explained that it is sometimes helpful to look at an example as a way of beginning to talk about our own circumstances.

We then told them that we were going to show them a short film clip from *Remember the Titans* that deals with the issue of racial integration in a community and that is based on a true story. To cue up the clip, we told them the basic story of the movie and what they would see in the clip. We made sure they understood what they would be viewing, who the characters were, and what the scene was.

Because it was a large group, we connected a video tape machine to an LCD (liquid crystal display) projector and showed the clip on a large screen. We also added external speakers so the sound was adequate for all to hear.

Following the viewing of the film clip, there were table discussions. We typed questions on a half-sheet of paper, put enough copies for each person in the group on each table, and asked that they discuss the questions after appointing a moderator for the group. The moderator was asked at the end of the time (15 minutes) to summarize the discussion for the larger group, so we all got an idea of the types of discussions that each table had.

Before starting a brief break, we passed out an article by Joan Richardson titled "Common Goals Override Individual Interests" and told the group that we would like everyone to read the introduction during the break (10 minutes). When we reconvened, the groups were instructed to break themselves up further, so that each of the six steps for dealing with conflict was read by someone in the group. Each member would explain his or her piece to the larger group at the table.

The rest of the evening was spent dealing with the first process piece: identifying the situation/question/problem that participants perceived in our community. Notes were kept on chart papers that were later collated and disseminated to the participants for the next meeting.

■ IN OTHER WORDS: QUOTES FOR EXTENDING THINKING AND CONVERSATIONS

Conflict itself is, of course, a sign of health as you would know if you ever met really apathetic people, really hopeless people, people who have given up hoping, striving, coping.

—Abraham Maslow

Every fight is on some level a fight between differing "angles of vision" illuminating the same truth.

—Mahatma Gandhi

I found one day in school a boy of medium size ill-treating a smaller boy. I expostulated, but he replied: "The bigs hit me, so I hit the babies; that's fair." In these words he epitomized the history of the human race.

—Bertrand Russell

The hottest places in Hell are reserved for those who in time of great moral crises maintain their neutrality.

—Dante Aleghieri

The harder the conflict, the more glorious the triumph. What we obtain too cheap, we esteem too lightly; it is dearness only that gives everything its value. I love the man that can smile in trouble, that can gather strength from distress and grow brave by reflection. 'Tis the business of little minds to shrink; but he whose heart is firm, and whose conscience approves his conduct, will pursue his principles unto death.

—Thomas Paine

Where all think alike, no one thinks very much.

—Walter Lippmann

Man must evolve for all human conflict a method which rejects revenge, aggression and retaliation. The foundation of such a method is love.

—Martin Luther King, Jr.

He who wrestles with us strengthens our nerves, and sharpens our skill. Our antagonist is our helper.

—Edmund Burke

First Myth: Conflict is negative. Nature uses conflict as a motivator for change.

—Thomas Crum

It is not enough to know that they see things differently. If you want to influence them, you also need to understand empathetically the power of their point of view and to feel the emotional force with which they believe in it.

—Roger Fisher & William Ury

ARTICLES FOR STUDY CIRCLES ■

Ackerman, R. H., & Maslin-Ostrowski, P. (2004). The wounded leader. *Educational Leadership, 61*(7), 28–32.

Amason, A., Thompson, K., Hochwater, W., & Harrison, A. (1995). Conflict: An important dimension in successful management teams. *Organizational Dynamics, 24*(2), 20–35.

Garmston, R. (1998). Graceful conflict. *Journal of Staff Development, 19*(3) [available at http://www.nsdc.org/library/publications/jsd/garmston193.cfm].

Heller, D. A. (2002). The power of gentleness. *Educational Leadership, 59*(8), 76–79.

Hergert, L. F. (1997). Turning diversity into a strength for decision making. *Journal of Staff Development, 18*(3).

McHenry, I. (2000). Conflict in schools. *Phi Delta Kappan, 82*(3), 223–227.

Mohr, N., & Dichter, A. (2001). Building a learning organization. *Phi Delta Kappan, 82*(10), 744–747.

Richardson, J. (1998). Common goals override individual interests. *Tools for Schools*, December [available at http://nsdc.org/library/publications/tools/tools12-98rich.cfm].

Sather, S., & Henze, R. (2001). Building relationships: Concrete steps show school leaders how to construct better interethnic relations. *Journal of Staff Development, 22*(2), 28.

Thompson, S. (2004). Leading from the eye of the storm. *Educational Leadership, 61*(7), 60–63.

Uline, C. L., Tschannen-Moran, M., & Perez, L. (2003). Constructive conflict: How controversy can contribute to school improvement. *Teachers College Record, 105*(5), 782–815.

Wagner, T. (1997). The new village commons—Improving schools together. *Educational Leadership, 54*(5), 25–28.

■ BOOKS FOR EXTENDED LEARNING

Brinkman, R., & Kirschner, R. (1994). *Dealing with people you can't stand.* New York: McGraw-Hill.

Crum, T. F. (1987). *The magic of conflict.* New York: Touchstone, Simon & Schuster.

Fisher, R., & Brown, S. (1988). *Getting together.* New York: Penguin.

Fisher, R., & Ury, W. (1981*). Getting to YES.* New York: Penguin.

Hurston, Z. N. (1937). *Their eyes were watching God* [Audiobook read by Michele-Denise Woods]. Prince Frederick, MD: Recorded Books, LLC. (1994)

Johnson, B. (1992). *Polarity management.* Amherst, MA: HRD Press.

Landsman, J. (2001). *A white teacher talks about race.* Lanham, MD: Scarecrow.

Ury, W. (1991). *Getting past no.* New York: Bantam.

Yeats, W. B. (1919). The Second Coming. Retrieved July 18, 2005, from http://www.online-literature.com/yeats/780/

Zander, B., & Zander, R. S. (2000). *The art of possibility.* Boston: Harvard Business School.

Film Clips That 2
Explore Courage
and Ethics

*Courage is that rare moment of unity between conscience, fear, and action,
when something deep within us strikes the flint of love, of honor, of duty, to
make the spark that fires our resolve. It's the moment—however brief or
singular—when we are our complete, best self, when we know with an almost
metaphysical certainty that we are right.*

—Senator John McCain, "In Search of Courage,"
Fast Company, September 2004, page 56

We adults do not talk much about courage or ethics in school or in training sessions. While courage and ethics are vital to the health of an individual, school, or district, we adults are normally too pressed to give these "soft" subjects much time and consideration. We violate Johann von Goethe's admonition that "things that matter most must never be at the mercy of things which matter least." Discussions of courage and ethics are usually reserved for history or English class in the struggles of characters, real and fictional, dealing with epic events. They can rise to prominence when yet another corporate executive, doctor, lawyer, priest spectacularly crosses the line by stealing, lying, or abusing people.

Yet we feel that courage and ethics might be two of the most important resources or assets we have. As courage and ethics are related to deeply held values, we think it is important to converse openly and regularly about such matters. Dialogues about ethics, courage, and values contribute to building a learning community with a common, shared, and enthusiastic vision.

Ethics—a sense of value of or commitment to more global, higher, or longer lasting features of life—generates deep commitment down to the soul's core. These values represent who we are, what we stand for, what we believe, and determine where we are headed—individually and collectively. They are what make us draw the line in the sand and say, "This far, and no farther." They are reflected in our goals in work and life.

Courage is the stiff backbone that helps lift us to the task of promoting, defending, and making good on our deep sense of purpose. Courage enables us to manifest something real out of a dream. Courage is not aggressive as much as it is assertive, that in the face of all this adversity we choose to stand here and reiterate our position or create something different. Courage is our intention to build for the future that which does not exist yet, making things better for those who come after us. Courage is the energy that gives substance and meaning to our ethics.

Courage must be a value that our society holds in high esteem. Look at all the books, movies, headlines, and so on, that mention courage. It seems like a value that many of us are drawn to. I (WO) take it that all this attention represents attempts to get next to, to understand, and to acquire courage simply by saying the word. Strange, isn't it? *Woman of Courage, Men of Courage, Profiles in Courage, Kids of Courage, Courage Under Fire, Red Badge of Courage, The Courage to Teach, The Courage to Remember*, and *The Courageous Followers*. We seem to recognize its importance, and we have benefited from those who have taken courageous steps.

A Google.com search turned up the following, searching on courage: about 5,920,000 hits for courage in just 0.19 seconds. If it were only as easy to find that much courage so quickly!

Ethics is similar. It is probably true that all professions have some sort of code of ethics or code of conduct. There are many codes of ethics—for schools, businesses, professions, nonprofits, and so on. In codes of ethics, beliefs are spelled out and expected behavior is defined. In other words, even if things get tough and there is much adversity, we will adhere to these concepts or codes and ways of behaving. We do this because it is the honorable thing to do, pointing to a higher or more universal human value or behavior. Where do we talk about what those codes are and what they mean to people we work with?

For all our expressed hopes, it looks for all the world like it is very difficult to live up to these higher ways. We are all too familiar with gross violations in the business world, in governments, and even in education. Lapses occur even in the world of religion, one of the last places you would expect to find such failure. Slips seem to occur in many areas of life, almost as if no one is immune, no matter how much we hope that when we ourselves are challenged we will behave consistently and ethically. Ethics are foundational in trust, relationships, and positive work cultures.

It seems to us that ethics and courage are tied together. Ethics gives us a framework to live up to or to begin behaving into the ethical standard, and courage is necessary because the world is a challenging place. As a school principal, I (WS) get invitations from parents, staff, and students to deviate from equitable and fair practice, sometimes at the expense of others. Ethics keeps me thinking about what is good for all students, and courage helps me make the case while standing on solid ground.

Are ethics and courage necessary? Where are they commonly found? How important are they to us personally and to our schools, other organizations, our way of life? How much practice do we need to get it right? And if we do it right, is there any guarantee that things will turn out all right? If not, why do it? Why does it take courage to speak up?

Think of examples of groupthink and how hard it is to say something that is not what the group wants to hear. There are many examples in business and education. It is about stepping up; it is about finding one's voice and having unusual clarity about what one wants, says, or does.

Courage and ethics are harder to come by in schools these days. The push to be customer service–oriented leads to more demands that may provide individuals with what they or their parents want while sacrificing the good of the whole. These issues will be increasingly important in a more diverse world and with more pressure to get ahead. Educators have been and will remain one of the most important groups to maintain balance and integrity and to honor all points of view. There will continue to be pressure for charter schools, private agencies, and independent organizations to give customers what they demand, sometimes at the expense of others.

If educators do not stand up for all students, for impoverished families, and promote democratic principles, who will? If schools are not based on democratic ideals, when and where will these beliefs be taught?

CLIPS ■

Clip: Commitment

Themes: Commitment, values, clear vision, action

Film Title & Synopsis: *A Lesson Before Dying* **(1999) (TV).** This made-for-television movie by HBO is an adaptation of Ernest J. Gaines's novel of the same name. Jefferson (Mekhi Phifer) is wrongly accused of murdering a white store owner in 1940s Louisiana. In his defense of Jefferson, arguing against a death sentence, his attorney (played by Sonny Shroyer) says, "You might just as soon put a hog in the 'lectric chair as this," stunning Jefferson into a deep depression and outraging and appalling his godmother, Miss Emma (Irma P. Hall). Jefferson is subsequently convicted and sentenced to death. Sensing the impact of the lawyer's words on Jefferson and being deeply offended by them herself, Miss Emma enlists the help of the community's teacher, Grant Wiggins (Don Cheadle), to convince Jefferson that he is a man, not a hog, so he can die honorably. Grant, Miss Emma, and others visit Jefferson frequently as the story unfolds.

Clip Setup: Grant, Miss Emma, and Jefferson's aunt, Tante Lou (Cicely Tyson), drive up to the house of Henri Pichot (Stuart Culpepper), brother-in-law of Sheriff Guidry (Frank Hoyt Taylor). Miss Emma's mission is to get Henri to persuade his sheriff brother-in-law, who is in charge of the jail where Jefferson is being held, to allow Grant to visit Jefferson regularly. Miss Emma wants Grant, over a period of time and before Jefferson is executed, to persuade and convince Jefferson of his humanity, neutralizing the impact of the defense attorney's reference to Jefferson being a hog.

Start Movie: 00:10:22 as Grant Wiggins drives down the long driveway to the house.

Stop Movie: 00:13:46 as Miss Emma tells Henri that she will be back to get an answer. The next scene opens in a bar where Grant meets his girl—Vivian Baptiste (Lisa Arrindell Anderson).

Approximate Length: 3:22

Questions for Discussion:

1. What did you notice in yourself and in the clip as you watched the scene?

2. Describe behaviors that Miss Emma exhibited that were evidence of her commitment or strong feeling.

3. What was effective about what she did?

4. Are there areas in your work environment where you have to be more assertive, stronger? Describe where they are and why you feel this way.

5. How can you or your team be more assertive? Describe key behaviors.

Why We Really Like This Clip: When Tante Lou says, "This ain't no ordinary day, Grant," to disarm Grant's anger at having to drive around to the back, she stakes out what looks like the wisest position, given that she clearly had a goal (getting permission for Grant to visit Jefferson in jail on a regular basis) that was not to be compromised. In other words, Tante Lou chose what battle she was going to fight at that moment, a choice many of us have had to make on the spot. We admire her clarity of purpose, even while she had expressed strongly her hope that Grant would never have to go through that back door another day in his life.

Miss Emma is clear when, in spite of Grant's confusion about what good he would do by seeing Jefferson ("I have no idea"), she persists in going after her goal of having Henri convince Sheriff Guidry to let Grant visit Jefferson. Further, Miss Emma would not be diverted by Mr. Henri as he pleads with her to "let the law have him." She perseveres by reminding Mr. Henri what she has done for the family, appealing to his sense of fairness. She argues him into submission and closes in by asking when she could expect an answer. Finally she says, in response to Henri's vagueness ("whenever I see him"), "I'll be back tomorrow." Now that is commitment and skill aimed at securing a result! Given the times and social conditions, we see Miss Emma's performance as an act of courage as well.

We see this clip as offering a chance for teams, departments, and schools to talk about dogged commitment to a goal. We see in this clip what it looks like, and there is an opportunity to help teams see what it would look like in their environments. As the challenges in schools and other organizations today are huge, teams can also face the issue of the courage it takes to persist in environments where the odds are overwhelmingly against success.

Notes:

_____

_____

_____

_____

_____

_____

_____

_____

Clip: Courage—I Am the President

Themes: Courage, character, values, dealing with opposition, finding one's self or voice

Film Title & Synopsis: *The American President* (1995). Andrew Shepherd (Michael Douglas) is an enormously popular president who is a widower. He and an environmental lobbyist, Sydney Ellen Wade (Annette Bening), fall for each other. As their romance becomes more public, both the press and rival Senator Bob Rumson (Richard Dreyfuss) mount intense criticism, causing his popularity to fall.

Clip Setup: President Shepherd finally steps up to his duty as a president and a person in a news conference.

Start Movie: 1:39:00 as the White House comes on the screen and the press secretary says, "Because the president feels there is no value in this kind of character debate."

Stop Movie: 1:44:22 as the president walks out of the pressroom.

Approximate Length: 5:18

Questions for Discussion:

1. What did you observe? What were your reactions?

2. What values does the president espouse? Listen and watch carefully for those that are both spoken and unspoken.

3. What are the reactions of various people in the room?

4. Think about your institution (team, department, school, district). What values do you espouse? Which are clearly articulated? Which

are there but hidden; that is, which are espoused but not followed by authentic behavior? Look for explanations under the answers to the questions.

5. How do we know President Andrew Shepherd means it?

6. In what ways can you "mean it" more authentically in your work environment? Describe the behavior.

Why We Really Like This Clip: Here is an example of a leader who thinks that if he ignores an issue, it will go away. The president does not want to get into a character debate during the reelection campaign, wanting instead to focus on economic and foreign issues. As the other side continues to focus on character, one of his aides, Louis (Michael J. Fox), takes a risk and challenges the president. Louis tells him that the reason this issue persists is because the other side is the only one talking. Louis challenges him to make his case to the American public.

In this scene, the president surprises the press conference by showing up and then taking the podium. He gives an impromptu speech that addresses his relationship with Sydney Wade and his commitment to solving problems, and he refocuses what the presidential campaign is and is not about. His frank and direct talk not only clarifies issues for the press but it also reenergizes his staff. The courage he demonstrates by taking the issues head-on may help others to create their own courageous moments.

Notes:

_____

_____

_____

_____

_____

_____

_____

_____

Clip: Dance of Defiance

Themes: Confrontation, values, father/son relationship, dealing with truth, strength of conviction

Film Title & Synopsis: *Billy Elliot* (2000). Eleven-year-old Billy Elliot (Jamie Bell) rejects boxing lessons at the gym and quite accidentally discovers a love and talent for dance. He struggles with his father (Gary

Lewis) and brother (Jamie Draven) (both of whom are involved in an ugly miners' strike), who ridicule Billy's love of dance.

Clip Setup: As Billy's father and his friends are walking in the street following a late-night Christmas celebration, they notice a light on in the boxing gym. When they investigate, they find Billy and his friend playing. Billy finds himself face to face with his father in the gym. He's been "caught" dancing, and Billy has the chance to stand up for what he believes. *Warning:* **This clip contains language that some may find offensive.**

Start Movie: 1:07:18 as Billy turns on the light in the dark gym as the door shuts behind him. His friend Michael (Stuart Wells) is standing in the middle of the gym freezing.

Stop Movie: 1:11:22 as Billy stands in the cold street after yelling, "Dad!" The next scene opens with his dad running down a street in a different section of town. A bush is decorated with Christmas lights.

Approximate Length: 4:02

Questions for Discussion:

1. As you think about the film clip, what stands out in your mind? Why?

2. The scene represents a clash of values, power, control, and courage. How do you see those elements play out in the scene? What are the clashes of values, power, and control in your team, school, or district?

3. How and why was violence averted?

4. If you were Billy's dad, where would you be off to? How would you deal with the situation?

5. What is your opinion about how they all dealt with the situation?

6. Do you see any parallels with or applications of any of the principles we observed in the clip in our own work environment? Think of values, standing up for what you believe, courage, ethics, power, and control.

Why We Really Like This Clip: We admire Billy's coaching ability with his friend Michael in the gym. Billy appears safe enough to share his special gifts and insights with his friend. At the same time, Billy seems intrigued at being able to teach his friend. When they break out in play we think it reminds us to have more fun with our art.

The moment when Billy comes face to face with his father is a moment we also face sometimes in our professional life. The question is, will we hide ourselves and our values, or will we have the courage to stand where we are and be authentic? Billy answers the question gracefully by dancing in front of his father rather than explaining, arguing, defending, or relenting.

Although we are fairly certain that the situation is not going exactly as he would like it to, Billy's dad displays courage as well by being open to his son's special difference. The dad's openness might easily have been squashed by his buddies, but he withstood whatever pressure he might have felt internally and externally and did what was in his heart according to his values. (Although you do not see it in this scene, when Billy's father abruptly left the gym, he headed to the dance teacher's house to make arrangements for Billy's lessons and talk about Billy's future in dance.)

Notes:

_____

_____

_____

_____

_____

_____

_____

Clip: Principle Versus Pragmatism

Themes: Ethics, short-/long-term view, perspectives, values, teaching

Film Title & Synopsis: *The Emperor's Club* **(2002).** The film traces the relationships of a dedicated classics teacher, William Hundert (Kevin Kline), and a troublesome student, Sedgewick Bell (Emile Hirsch as a kid and Joel Gretsch as the older Bell). Hundert is a classics teacher at St. Benedictus School for Boys, a private school for rich kids. The parents of the kids are people of influence. Bell's father is a U.S. Senator and somewhat cold and indifferent to the youngster, causing him to act out in bothersome ways in class, challenging Hundert. Every year, Hundert runs a popular contest at the school based on testing the students' knowledge of Roman history—Hundert asks the questions and the students answer until a winner emerges. The winner enters the prestigious and long-standing "Emperor's Club" with much pomp, honor, and esteem. Hundert discovers Bell cheating, but he does not confront him and instead defeats Bell by asking a question he knew Bell would find impossible. Years later, at a reunion sponsored by the wealthy Bell, a replay of the contest is featured. Hundert again discovers Bell cheating and again is able to defeat him with an impossible question. But this time Hundert confronts Bell.

Clip Setup: Sedgewick Bell grows up to be a wealthy man. He decides to replay as an adult the "Emperor's Club" competition he had as a student that he almost won—by cheating. Although Hundert catches on to Sedgwick's mischief, he keeps it to himself and successfully keeps Bell from winning the championship by manipulating the questions asked.

So Bell, as a wealthy adult about to announce his candidacy for the Senate, flies all the class members to a swank country club for a weekend party where they would replay the competition and to announce his candidacy. Oddly enough, the competition plays out in the same manner as the one when Bell was a student. Bell attempts to cheat, Hundert catches on, Hundert stays quiet to keep from blowing Bell's cover, and Hundert successfully keeps Bell from winning the championship by manipulating the questions asked. This time, however, there is a private confrontation between Bell and Hundert. *Warning:* **This clip contains language that some may find offensive.**

Start Movie: 1:32:08 as Hundert is bent over a sink washing his face (as if cleansing his soul) and Bell comes into the men's room and says, "Here you are!" Hundert is dealing with the weight of his conscience, having observed Bell cheating to win the contest at a class reunion, just as he had done when he was a young student.

Stop Movie: 1:35:55 as Bell walks away from Hundert, going after his son, who has left the men's room after hearing the conversation.

Approximate Length: 3:48

Questions for Discussion:

1. What did you observe? What can you say about both men from your observation of the scene?

2. Hundert indicates that he will not go out (into the public) and expose Bell as a liar and a cheat because, "I am a teacher." What did Hundert mean by that? To what extent do you agree or disagree with his position?

3. Further, Hundert says to Bell, "I failed you as a teacher." How much do you agree with that statement? To what extent can a teacher be responsible for a student's moral development? Intellectual development?

4. Hundert offers one last "lecture" to his student: "All of us, at some point, are forced to look at ourselves in the mirror and see who we really are. And when that day comes for you, Sedgewick, you'll be confronted with a life lived without virtue, without principle and for that I pity you. End of lesson." Bell responds with, "What can I say, Mr. Hundert. Who gives a shit? Honestly, who out there gives a shit

about your principles and your virtues?! . . . I live in the real world where people do what they need to do to get what they want. And if it's lying and it's cheating, so be it." What side would you take in this conversation? Why? And to what extent is each right?

5. What ethical issues or tensions exist in your work environment? What are the issues and positions? How would you resolve the tension?

Why We Really Like This Clip: Finally, Hundert gets the courage to confront Bell and himself. We wonder how things might have been different had Hundert confronted Bell when he was a student. Of course we will never know, and neither will Hundert, and that is his burden. It was a missed opportunity for both of them that might have changed the results. It reminds us to be aware of the choices we have when situations arise that require courage. Although it may be the more uncomfortable course of action, we believe it to be the healthier course to declare and follow our principles.

We also enjoy the twist at the end of the scene, when Bell's son reveals himself. It reminds us of the importance of living congruent and authentic lives, even if no one is watching. How will Bell explain his hypocrisy to his son? Which of Bell's values—his son or winning—has greater weight? It raises questions for us as well. How closely do we live our principles? How would we explain ourselves to our children?

Notes:

_____

_____

_____

_____

_____

_____

_____

Clip: Truth Telling

Themes: Truth telling, honesty, friendship, leaving

Film Title & Synopsis: *Good Will Hunting* (1997). Will Hunting (Matt Damon) is a naturally gifted math genius. This becomes apparent when

Hunting solves an arcane equation posted on a hallway white board by a famous MIT math professor, Gerald Lambeau (Stellan Skarsgård), as a challenge to his students. Will, working as a janitor at the school, solves the equation, to everyone's surprise. Professor Lambeau, seeing Will's gift for math, commits to helping him turn his life from carousing with his buddy Chuckie Sullivan (Ben Affleck) to more intellectual pursuits. Professor Lambeau finds Will difficult and enlists the help of Sean Maguire (Robin Williams), a Boston psychologist whom he knew years ago in school.

Clip Setup: Will and Chuckie have a profound and courageous conversation about their futures as they share a beer and a smoke on the construction site where they work. *Warning:* **This clip contains language that some may find offensive.**

Start Movie: 1:40:42 as Professor Lambeau says, "OK. Fine." and hangs up the phone. The scene shifts to a construction site as Will and Chuckie have a beer, a smoke, and a conversation at the front of the pickup truck on the construction site.

Stop Movie: 1:43:41 as the scene shifts from the construction site to Sean's office and Professor Lambeau says, "This is a disaster, Sean."

Approximate Length: 3:01

Questions for Discussion:

1. What did you make of the clip? What did you observe in yourself and on screen?

2. How do these guys (Will and Chuckie) see the world and their futures?

3. How is Chuckie's truth telling to Will an act of courage? In what ways was Chuckie soft? In what ways was he tough?

4. How do we know that Chuckie means what he says?

5. What is the impact of Chuckie's clarity on Will?

6. Thinking about your work environment (company, school, department, team, etc.), where do you need more truth telling? Where do you need to be softer and how? Where do you need to be tougher and how? How could you contribute to starting the courageous conversation?

Why We Really Like This Clip: Sometimes the most difficult things to say are the best things to say. What we like is the organic nature of the talk—it just happened, although obviously both had thought about the topic before. We also admire Chuckie's courage in speaking directly, assertively, and compassionately to Will, clearly freeing Will from the entrapments of the environment, including their friendship. Clearly this was a different kind of a conversation, a fierce conversation (see the great work, *Fierce Conversations* [Scott, 2002]) rather than the conversational coma that often characterizes our interactions.

We think that the clip invites teams or workgroups to tell the truth in a caring and compassionate way, just like Chuckie did with Will. Telling the truth without blame or judgment is a skill worth practicing as it has a profound impact, forcing people to a new level of reality. What are we not saying that needs to be said? What does our future look like? How are we going to get there? What strengths do we have? We think such thoughtful and reflective conversations are necessary to make stronger, more successful, and more rewarding organizations.

Notes:

_____

_____

_____

_____

_____

_____

_____

_____

Clip: Faith and What You Believe

Themes: Vision, risk, commitment, faith

Film Title & Synopsis: *Indiana Jones and the Last Crusade* **(1989).** This is the third (and final) Indiana Jones film. It features Indiana Jones (Harrison Ford) and his somewhat difficult father, Professor Henry Jones (Sean Connery), fighting Nazis (and other collectors) to find and secure the Holy Grail, giver of everlasting life.

Clip Setup: Walter Donovan (Julian Glover), a wealthy and noted collector of antiquities, has shot Professor Jones as a way of motivating Indiana Jones to make the final journey through dangerous obstacles to obtain the Holy Grail, the grail being the only thing that can save Indy's wounded father.

Start Movie: 1:43:17 just after Indiana Jones reaches for a handkerchief to apply to his father's wound. Donovan, the bad guy with a gun, says, "You can't save him when you're dead. The healing power of the grail is the only thing that will save him now. It's time to ask yourself, what do you believe?"

Stop Movie: 1:48:50 just after Jones throws dust onto the invisible bridge so others who follow may see and go to help him find his way back.

Approximate Length: 5:35

Questions for Discussion:

1. Donovan says to Indy, "It's time to ask yourself, what do you believe?"
   a. To what extent does a crisis have to be present to answer this question?
   b. Indy is being asked to act on his beliefs or values, to make good on them. What are your most prominent or important values? How are you, in your environment (company, school, department, team, etc.), asked to make good on your values?

2. Notice how important Indy's thinking about language is to his success in getting through. Reflect on your environment for a moment. What labels, concepts, processes, or goals do you need to think more clearly about to improve your chances of understanding and success? Explain.

3. Indy is challenged to make a "leap of faith." His father hopes to guide Indy by saying, "You must believe, boy, you must . . . believe." To Indy's surprise, there is "something" there, something to stand on, that was invisible from his perspective. What is the lesson here? How can you use these lessons in your work, individually and as a group?

4. What do you think: Was Indy marking his way back, or was he doing it for others to follow, when he threw dust on the invisible bridge? To what extent can you make the invisible visible for others? Why might that be important to your work together?

Why We Really Like This Clip: What a challenge—"It's time to ask yourself, what do you believe?" That is a question we need to ask ourselves over and over again in our schools and other organizations. We need to talk with each other about that and carefully analyze how congruent our actions and policies are with those beliefs. We think the question about what we believe is a great place to start and continue discussions in our teams, departments, and schools/districts—and to tie our beliefs to action.

We also think that the clip challenges us to have the conversations before the crisis, when the gun of competition, chaos, or dislocation is pointed at your school, district, or other organizations. If we have the conversations frequently and regularly, we believe we can avoid being caught by the crisis.

We also saw the extraordinary effort that Indy made in trying to interpret the clues he had as he proceeded. He succeeds at the first obstacle only when he expands his concept of "penitent" to mean humble, kneeling. At the second obstacle, he almost loses it because of information his father had and Indy did not remember—that in the Latin alphabet Jehovah begins with an "I." We see a parallel here with schools and organizations trying to figure out, with only fragmentary, incomplete information, what their next moves should be. As we can see in the clip, mapping our future course is hard work that requires creativity, moving us beyond single, rote definitions and concepts. We would also add that this work should not be done alone (Indy had no choice). The more information available in the form of diverse ideas, views, and perspectives, the better the decision is likely to be.

Finally, there is the business of risk taking and faith. Indy says, "It's impossible. Nobody can jump this." And, of course, he is right. Nobody can jump it. What assumptions is he making? While no one can jump it, it can be crossed. "It's a leap of faith!" is based on scanty information that pays off as he discovers what he cannot see from his angle. As all good explorers do, he marks the way by throwing dust on the path, making it visible for others to see or for him to find his way back. We think that leaps of faith are sometimes required to make a success of endeavors. Organizations and plans can become paralyzed by waiting for all the necessary information to come in—sometimes you have to go with what you have and make the best of it.

Notes:

_____

_____

_____

_____

_____

_____

_____

Clip: Fighting for Lost Causes

Themes: Values, fighting for lost causes, persistence

Film Title & Synopsis: *Mr. Smith Goes to Washington* (1939). Jefferson Smith (Jimmy Stewart) is appointed to the U.S. Senate by Governor Hubert "Happy" Hopper (Guy Kibbee) following the death of the incumbent senator. The governor and party machine believed that Smith, a leader of the scout-like Boy Rangers, is naïve and easy to manipulate by the senior senator from that state, Senator Joseph Harrison Paine (Claude Rains).

Clip Setup: Smith, a newly appointed U.S. Senator, shares a conversation with the other and senior senator from his state, the veteran Senator Joseph Harrison Paine, in a private train car as they head for Washington, D.C., together for the first time.

Start Movie: 00:14:45 as the train speeds the newly appointed Senator Smith and the veteran Senator Paine toward Washington. Both men are seated in a rail car facing one another. Senator Smith, pulling out a paper from his briefcase, says, "Well, it isn't much, but if you insist . . ."

Stop Movie: 00:16:40 as Smith says, "One man by himself can't get very far, can he?" Paine answers, "No." The scene changes to Washington, D.C., as the new senator says, "Washington, huh?"

Approximate Length: 1:53

Questions for Discussion:

1. How would you define lost causes? What are some common examples of lost causes? See if you can identify any lost causes in your work environment and explain why you see them as such. How important are they?

2. Why would a person believe that the only causes worth fighting for are the lost causes?

3. Where would you draw the line between fighting for lost causes, persistence, and being an obstructionist?

4. What are the benefits and the drawbacks of fighting for lost causes?

5. For all the talk of and admiration for lost causes, there is an almost paradoxical view expressed by Senator Smith when he says to Senator Paine, "I suppose, Mr. Paine, when a fella bucks up against a big organization like that, one man by himself can't get very far, can he?" So, if you cannot get very far as a single person, why buck the system? To what extent do you believe a person can be effective in bucking the organization?

6. What skills in your work environment might help avoid the polarization and immobility implied in words like "lost causes," "obstruction," and "fighting"?

7. To what extent is courage needed for fighting for lost causes?

Why We Really Like This Clip: We like this clip a lot because it reminds us of the importance of fighting for lost causes. Doing so takes courage— the courage of one's convictions and the courage to keep going in the face of inconceivable odds. Too often in organizational discussions we give up or in too easily, without giving the matter the full and complete interrogation it requires. We believe that doing so plays to our weaknesses, not our strengths. Compliance over creativity and competence is reinforced. Vigorous challenges lead to improved decisions, and vigorous challenges can often feel like lost causes.

As Fullan and Hargreaves point out in *What's Worth Fighting for Out There* (1998), fighting for lost causes may take the form of "not giving up on difficult students" (p. 120). Or it may mean "not giving in to governments whose reforms don't have students' interests at heart" (p. 120). We think it could also apply to questioning the norms of the myriad of taken-for-granted interactions and processes in our organizational life. The clip offers the opportunity for teams to think about what they are really doing.

Notes:

_____

_____

_____

_____

_____

_____

_____

Clip: Meeting Re: Accreditation

Themes: Leadership, truth telling, honesty, conflict, values

Film Title & Synopsis: *Stand and Deliver* (1988). Based on a true story, Jaime Escalante (Edward James Almos) is a high school math teacher who beats the odds with kids from the barrio in Los Angeles. Challenging the expectations of the staff, the community, and the college board, the students buckle down to work hard and pass the Advanced Placement Calculus Test, defying common beliefs.

Clip Setup: We observe a meeting where the principal is trying to coax the group into positive steps to avoid losing accreditation. The scene progresses past the meeting to Escalante's classroom, where he talks about reality, expectations, and *ganas* (desire).

Start Movie: 00:17:48 as Escalante quietly walks into a meeting already in progress, in which the principal is talking about a loss of accreditation.

Stop Movie: 00:20:41 as Escalante says, "No questions? Good!" Angel's (Lou Diamond Phillips) friend comes to the door of the classroom (in the middle of class) and motions for him to come into the hall.

Approximate Length: 2:54

Questions for Discussion:

1. What do you hear in the following statements from the scene:
    a. "I don't want to be the principal of the first school in the history of Los Angeles to lose its accreditation."
    b. "I'm the last person to say that this math department couldn't improve. If you want higher test scores, start by changing the economic level of this community."
    c. "I don't think I should be teaching math next semester. I mean, I was hired to be a phys. ed. instructor."
    d. "As I said before, we lack the resources to implement the changes the district demands."
    e. "You can't teach logarithms to illiterates. These kids come to us with barely a seventh-grade education. Now, there isn't a teacher in this room that isn't doing everything he possibly can."

2. How would you deal with the situation?

3. To what extent is it an act of courage for Escalante to say, "I'm not. I could teach more"? What acts of courage do you believe are required in your work environment?

4. What is being expressed when the math department chair says, "I'm sure Mr. Escalante has good intentions, but he's only been here a few months"?

5. How would you describe the values you see in the scene? To what extent are you clear about your values in your school and district?

Why We Really Like This Clip: We really like this clip because it portrays the all-too-familiar reality of faculty discussions. There are innumerable ideas about how to produce results in schools. The task of producing results is often compromised by adult situations, as in, "I don't think I should be teaching math next semester. I mean, I was hired to be a phys. ed. instructor." The question confronting the group is how to overcome inertia and get on with a direction, a goal, and action. Escalante had the *ganas* (desire) and courage to challenge the norms and assumptions in the meeting with a different and accountable point of view. It is interesting to us that, in the process of Escalante doing so, the other participants seemed to stop, interest was aroused, and he had an opportunity to explain his point of view, albeit for only a short time in the clip. His courage created an opening to reconsider what the group believed and what their actions would be in the future. We wonder how different our school houses and organizations could be if there was more *ganas* (desire), interest, and courage. The clip provides an opening for teams, departments, schools, and organizations to talk about courage in their environments.

Notes:

_____

_____

_____

_____

_____

_____

_____

Clip: You Can't Handle the Truth

Themes: Conflict, digging for the truth, accommodation, duty, courage.

Film Title & Synopsis: *A Few Good Men* (1992). When a U.S. soldier dies at Gitmo (Guantanamo Naval Air Station in Cuba), Lieutenant Daniel Kaffee (Tom Cruise) is appointed to defend the two accused, stubborn, by-the-book marines—Private First Class Louden Downey (James Marshall) and Lance Corporal Harold W. Dawson (Wolfgang Bodison). Lieutenant Commander JoAnne Galloway (Demi Moore) is hired by Downey's aunt to represent him as well. It seems Private First Class Santiago was given a "code red"—where soldiers in a unit take it on themselves to discipline screwups so as to motivate them to do better. In the "code red" process, Santiago is accidentally killed. The essential question is, was the "code red" given as an order by higher ups, or was it done simply by the two accused marines? While conducting their investigation to defend the two marines, Kaffee and Galloway sense that Colonel Nathan R. Jessup (Jack Nicholson), a well-connected, politically savvy marine who is rumored to be headed for appointment to the National Security Council, is not telling all he knows and that Lieutenant Jonathan Kendrick (Kiefer Sutherland) and Lieutenant Colonel Matthew Markinson (J. T. Walsh) are helping Jessup cover up the truth. Because of military law, Kaffee needs to be careful with his questioning to avoid charges that could be leveled against him by Jessup if he is wrong.

Clip Setup: This is perhaps the most famous scene in the film. Kaffee is questioning Jessup's seemingly contradictory orders, leaving open the possibility that Jessup ordered the "code red." The guilt or innocence of the two charged marines hangs on Jessup's testimony. *Warning:* **This clip contains language that some may find offensive.**

Start Movie: 2:04:36 when Jessup has just asked if Kaffee is clear and Kaffee says, "Crystal." Start the scene as Kaffee says to Jessup, leaning toward him, "Colonel, I've just one more question before I call Airman O'Malley and Airman Rodriquez."

Stop Movie: 2:10:02 as Jessup leaves the courtroom accompanied by MPs (Military Police).

Approximate Length: 5:30

Questions for Discussion:

1. What did you see? What struck you about the scene?

2. To what extent is Jessup right—that we can't handle the truth—that we trade security for looking the other way on some matters?

3. Think about your work environment. What trades, accommodations, or bargains do you make as a department, team, school, or district that are somewhat bothersome?

4. How would you characterize the worldview of each of the characters?

5. In your opinion, is it ever acceptable to withhold the truth? Explain.

6. What truths are you aware of in your work environment that are not being expressed or are being withheld? What is the impact of that on people and the school or district?

Why We Really Like This Clip: Getting at the truth is sometimes risky. The clip reminds us of the courage it takes to keep challenging authority, reflecting on what answers were given, and coming back again with additional points and questions. It is troublesome that Jessup thinks that, because "people" want and need him "on the wall" defending U.S. boundaries and integrity, he can disobey the law, and that his special position of being "on the wall" and protecting our civilization from evil grants him special treatment. His attitude toward others is contemptuous, so while he is protecting the homeland, he feels contempt for the people, processes, and laws he is defending. The scene also raises the issue of what courage is. For some, Jessup is acting courageously by running a tight ship and remaining vigilantly "on the wall." For others, Kaffee is more courageous for going so steadfastly after the truth. What differentiates the two? To what extent can questions of this nature be either/or, black/white, right/wrong?

Notes:

_____

_____

_____

_____

_____

_____

_____

■ FIELD WORK: HOW DOES THIS WORK IN REAL TIME WITH REAL PEOPLE? STAND AND DELIVER

Recently we were invited to an eastern state to do some training for principals and department leaders. The overriding issue that emerged was that district mandates were not in line with what these principals and department leaders thought about learning and teaching students. The question was how to tell district leaders without making their bosses mad. Nobody wanted to do a CLM (career limiting move).

Initially we talked about what we believe about student learning, what the building educators' main purpose is for being in this career, and what the non-negotiables are for a strong and vibrant school culture that supports learning for students and staff.

We also presented information given by Roger Fisher and William Ury in their book, _Getting to Yes_ (1991), in which they discuss the concept of BATNA (best alternative to a negotiated agreement). In other words, what is your bottom line, or what will you fight for? Allowing time for people to develop their personal and professional BATNAs was necessary in order to have a collective discussion. Once we got the group's BATNAs, we turned our attention to the issue of courage to advance their beliefs and values.

Then, we told them we were going to watch a video of Michael Douglas playing the role of Andrew Shepherd, the president of the United States, in the movie _The American President._ Throughout the movie the president is being attacked by an opponent for having a romantic relationship with an environmental lobbyist. The president hopes the opponent will just go away or that people will not believe him. However, the approval ratings of the president are dropping because he is not responding.

The clip that we showed is of the president finally responding (having discovered his BATNA) at a press conference, assertively and articulately making his case. The clip ends with the powerful and firm statement, "My name is Andrew Shepherd and I am the president."

After the clip we asked groups of four to five people to write a "laser talk" to give to the people in charge. A laser talk is about three minutes maximum, about the time you would have in an elevator if you were riding with a person you wanted time with and now had. A laser talk has points that you want to make in a short time. Laser talks should be crafted in the form of observations—just data, not judgment. The laser talk ends with a request, something you want the person(s) to do. It is not enough to complain or tell people what is wrong. Courage is also coming with a solution or request for the person. What are the most important things you want to say? Remember, it must be to the point, given quickly, and end with a request.

We then gave the participants an article from the *Minnesota School Boards Association Journal* (Sommers, 2004) titled "Everyday Heroes and Sheroes: Courage to Ride the Waves of Change Without Drowning" and had them read it. This article is about the courage to do what is right and not what is always popular or easy. The participants then gave their talks to another group. With feedback, they refined their laser talks.

Some participants decided they would find their supervisors and give their laser talk that day or the next. It is important to deliver the laser talk without blame or judgment. If there is a "get you" message, it will usually result in a backlash or negative consequence.

IN OTHER WORDS: ■
QUOTES FOR EXTENDING
THINKING AND CONVERSATIONS

Moral excellence comes about as a result of habit. We become just by doing just acts, temperate by doing temperate acts, brave by doing brave acts.

—Aristotle

Courage is the first of human qualities because it is the quality which guarantees all others.

—Winston Churchill

Dare to be naive.

—Buckminster Fuller

Creativity requires the courage to let go of certainties.

—Erich Fromm

I long to accomplish great and noble tasks, but it is my chief duty to accomplish humble tasks as though they were great and noble. The world is moved along, not only by the mighty shoves of its heroes, but also by the aggregate of the tiny pushes of each honest worker.

—Helen Keller

Patience and perseverance have a magical effect before which difficulties disappear and obstacles vanish.

—John Quincy Adams

Moral cowardice that keeps us from speaking our minds is as dangerous to this country as irresponsible talk. The right way is not always the popular and easy way. Standing for right when it is unpopular is a true test of moral character.

—Margaret Chase Smith

The best way out is always through.

—Robert Frost

To dare is to lose one's footing momentarily. To not dare is to lose oneself.

—Soren Kierkegaard

Cautious, careful people, always casting about to preserve their reputation and social standing, never can bring about a reform. Those who are really in earnest must be willing to be anything or nothing in the world's estimation, and publicly and privately, in season and out, avow their sympathy with despised and persecuted ideas and their advocates, and bear the consequences.

—Susan B. Anthony

To go against the dominant thinking of your friends, of most of the people you see every day, is perhaps the most difficult act of heroism you can perform.

—Theodore H. White

Personal mastery teaches us to choose. Choosing is a courageous act: picking the results and actions which you will make into your destiny.

—Peter Senge

Definition of courage: "Grace under pressure."

—Ernest Hemingway

Whatever you do, you need courage. Whatever course you decide upon, there is always someone to tell you that you are wrong. There are always difficulties arising that tempt you to believe your critics are right. To map out a course of action and follow it to an end requires some of the same courage that a soldier needs. Peace has its victories, but it takes brave men and women to win them.

—Ralph Waldo Emerson

Courage is not the lack of fear. It is acting in spite of it.

—Mark Twain

God grant me the Serenity to accept the things I cannot change, the Courage to change the things I can and the Wisdom to know the difference.

—Serenity prayer (Reinhold Niebuhr)

You gain strength, courage and confidence by every experience in which you really stop to look fear in the face. You are able to say to yourself, "I have lived through this horror. I can take the next thing that comes along." You must do the thing you think you cannot do.

—Eleanor Roosevelt

ARTICLES FOR STUDY CIRCLES ■

Brooks, M. G., & Brooks, J. G. (1999). The courage to be a constructivist. *Educational Leadership, 57*(3), 18–24.

Glickman, C. D. (2002). The courage to lead. *Educational Leadership, 59*(8), 41–44.

Heifetz, R. A., & Linsky, M. (2004). When leadership spells danger. *Educational Leadership, 61*(7), 33–37.

McCabe, D. L. (2004). Ten principles of academic integrity for faculty. *Change, 36*(3), 12–15.

Palmer, P. J. (1992). Divided no more: A movement approach to educational reform. *Change Magazine, 24*(2), 10–17 [available online at http://www.teacher formation.org/html/rr/index.cfm under "Related Writings"].

Palmer, P. J. (1993). Good talk about good teaching: Improving teaching through conversation and community. *Change Magazine, 25*(6), 8–13 [available online at http://www.teacherformation.org/html/rr/index.cfm under "Related Writings"].

Sommers, W. (2004, November-December). Everyday heroes and sheroes: Courage to ride the waves of change without drowning. *Minnesota School Boards Association Journal 57*(3), 16.

Trigg, R. L. (1997). The art of successful leadership. *Educational Leadership, 27*(3), 8–11.

BOOKS FOR EXTENDED LEARNING ■

Arrien, A. (1993). *The four-fold way: Walking paths of the warrior, teacher, healer, and visionary.* New York: HarperCollins.

Blanchard, K., & Peale, N. V. (1988). *The power of ethical management.* New York: Fawcett Crest.

Block, P. (1993). *Stewardship—Choosing service over self-interest*. San Francisco: Berrett-Koehler.

Bolman, L. G., & Deal, T. E. (1995). *Leading with soul*. San Francisco: Jossey-Bass.

Cashman, K. (1998). *Leadership from the inside out*. Provo, UT: Executive Excellence Publishing.

Catford, L., & Ray, M. (1991). *The path of the everyday hero*. Los Angeles: Jeremy Tarcher.

Chaleff, I. (1995). *The courageous follower*. San Francisco: Berrett-Koehler.

Covey, S. R. (1990). *Principle-centered leadership*. New York: Simon & Schuster.

DePree, M. (1997). *Leading without power: Finding hope in serving community*. San Francisco: Jossey-Bass

Fisher, R., & Ury, W. (1991). *Getting to yes*. New York: Penguin.

Fullan, M., & Hargreaves, A. (1998). *What's worth fighting for out there*. New York: Teachers College Press.

Hamel, G. (2000). *Leading the revolution*. Boston: Harvard Business School Press.

Hay, L. L. (1991). *The power is within you*. Carson, CA: Hay House.

Kouzes, J. M., & Posner, B. Z. (1993). *Credibility*. San Francisco: Jossey-Bass.

Machado, L. A. (1980). *The right to be intelligent*. Oxford, England: Pergamon.

Rivers, F. (1996). *The way of the owl*. San Francisco: HarperCollins.

Scott, S. (2002). *Fierce conversations*. New York: Penguin.

Terry, R. W. (1993). *Authentic leadership: Courage in action*. San Francisco: Jossey-Bass.

Thomas, K. W. (2000). *Intrinsic motivation at work*. San Francisco: Berrett-Koehler.

Film Clips That Explore Persistence, Commitment, and Values

3

What man actually needs is not a tensionless state but rather the striving and struggling for some goal worthy of him. What he needs is not the discharge of tension at any cost, but the call of a potential meaning waiting to be fulfilled by him.

—Victor Frankl

The late Ray Kroc of McDonald's Corporation said that persistence was the most important trait for workers. Persistence is the first "Habit of Mind" that Dr. Art Costa and Dr. Bena Kallick write about in their work for schools. Why? Well, without some persistence, people do not stay with projects, especially when problems arise. Persistence helps to overcome the impulsiveness that causes more errors in judgment and negative behavior. We see children and adults who will not stick with something but jump to whatever is new. Novelty is important, especially to creating new ideas and products. Developing persistence is also important to follow-through, to fully implement plans, and to see a project to the end.

The literature is filled with examples of researchers with persistence, from finding cures for diseases to building better mousetraps. Charles Garfield, in his book *Peak Performers*, says that knowing when to stay with a project is very intelligent. He also recognizes there is a time to abandon a plan, too. In James Collins's book, *Good to Great*, the concept of the fox and the hedgehog is used. This is a perfect example of the fox that jumps from one thing to another while the hedgehog keeps his focus and stays the course. Obviously, there is a need for both types in organizations. The key is knowing which type is needed when.

It takes persistence for research chemists and bioengineers to find new drugs to fight illness. Many times they do not know what they are looking for. It is like doing a jigsaw puzzle without having the picture on the box to use as a guide. Persistence keeps scientists going when there is no end in sight.

We also want adults to model for students, managers to model for employees, and professionals to model for their clients that continuing to find ways to solve problems is a good thing. In education, for example, when we try a new method of teaching, in what we call the "implementation dip," we evaluate the results. The results of anything new are not high because we are still growing accustomed to a new way of operating. In many schools and school districts we give up too early, try something else new, and end up back in the same place. It takes persistence to see a project through, to collect data and make a good decision on whether to continue.

We think that having young people show commitment to ideals, processes, and others is an important trait to develop. Adults in the workplace must demonstrate the same kind of commitment to each other to build healthy, strong environments. Healthy workplaces take time, energy, and consistent values. All employees must be committed to shared and articulated organizational values. When the occasional value breakdown occurs, we must commit ourselves to persisting, even when it is not easy. As the expression goes, "What is easy isn't always right and being right isn't always easy."

When our organizations publish strong values, speak about their importance to the workplace, and then act in alignment with those values, that will lead to a healthy group that is clear about how to operate. Yes, we need mission and vision. However, we also need values, which are the overt behaviors that affirm or dissuade people about our commitment to the mission and vision. Mission, vision, and values are a three-legged stool that provides a base for the organization. Persistence is the engine that drives our practice, even in the face of extraordinary challenges.

■ CLIPS

Clip: Failure Is Not an Option

Themes: Commitment, determination, action, persistence, verve

Film Title & Synopsis: *Apollo 13* **(1995).** Astronauts Jim Lovell (Tom Hanks), Fred Haise (Bill Paxton), and Jack Swigert (Kevin Bacon) and a ground crew led by Ken Mattingly (Gary Sinise) and Gene Kranz (Ed Harris) struggle to save the crew on a crippled space ship that is 205,000 miles from earth on its way to the moon in 1970. An explosion onboard has crippled the mother ship. They must figure out a way to stay alive and return to earth with only the dwindling resources onboard.

Clip Setup: In this scene, the ground crew begins thinking about how to get the astronauts home. They discover that power is everything and that the spaceship will have to be virtually shut down to conserve energy for reentry. Gene Kranz orders a thorough review of all circuits, switches, and so on to determine where energy can be saved. His determination is expressed when he says, "We never lost an American in space and we're sure as hell not going to lose one on my watch. Failure is not an option!"

Start Movie: 1:14:46 as Kranz picks up the chalk, begins to write on the chalkboard, and says, "So you're telling me that you can only give our guys 45 hours?"

Stop Movie: 1:16:47 as Kranz issues orders to squeeze every possible amp out of the system and says, "Failure is not an option!"

Approximate Length: 2:00

Questions for Discussion:

1. As you watched the film, what did you notice or observe in yourself or on the screen?

2. What would you say the general attitude was when Kranz says, "Gentlemen, that's not acceptable"?

3. There was no second-guessing the gentleman who said, "Power is everything." He said he had been looking at the data for an hour. They trusted him and his numbers. Thinking about your environment, what would you say the level of trust is in your school or district? Department or team? What impact does the level of trust have on a school/district?

4. Gene Kranz lays out the tasks ahead of the team. The problem seems complicated and difficult. Why is persistence a necessary ingredient for success? How important is having a goal(s) to the practice of persistence?

5. What would you say are some of the upsides to persistence? What caution would you give people about persistence?

6. How would you rate your team, school, or district with regard to persistence? Explain your reasoning leading to your conclusions.

7. This is clearly a team effort. To what extent is your team, department, school, or district making a team effort? How does the level of "teamness" impact your work, your success, and the success of your school or district?

Why We Really Like This Clip: When Kranz brings the ground crew together there is wringing of hands, a feeling of possibly giving up, and a sense of "we don't know what to do." Kranz refocuses the ground crew on a larger goal: bringing the flight crew home successfully. He focuses them by saying they have never lost anyone yet and it is not going to happen on his watch. When he says, "Failure is not an option!", he is drawing a line in the sand. Kranz will not accept anything less than success.

Watch the faces of the crew as Kranz is talking. They seem to be saying, "We will solve this, quit talking about it, and get into action." Sometimes we need a leader to reidentify the goal, provide hope that attainment is possible, and create the commitment to press on. People and groups sometimes stop just before they are successful. A leader must provide positive statements about persisting in the face of difficult odds. People follow the behavior that leaders model. Leaders lead by example.

Notes:

_____

_____

_____

_____

_____

_____

_____

Clip: One Thing

Themes: Values, self-knowledge, one's journey

Film Title & Synopsis: *City Slickers* **(1991).** We are told that the Buddhists have a saying: When the student is ready, the teacher appears. In this clip, the students could be three male friends who are having a middle-age crisis at the same time and decide to take a two-week trip together to herd cattle the old-fashioned way. Mitch Robbins (Billy Crystal) is a radio ad man who is beginning to feel his age, is not particularly interested in anything, and is losing his sense of humor. Phil Berquist's (Daniel Stern) wife walks out on him after she finds out he had an affair with a very young employee of his. And Ed Furillo (Bruno Kirby) is simply drifting, searching for meaning. Our teacher appears as Curly (Jack Palance), a tough, seasoned trail boss. The story unfolds as they drive a herd of cattle from New Mexico to Colorado in the traditional way: on horseback, over a dusty trail, with few modern conveniences.

Clip Setup: There has been a stampede caused by Mitch—he spooked the herd by grinding coffee beans in a battery-operated grinder. When Curly finally stops the herd, he tells the group that he and Mitch are going to go after the strays and bring them back. During this brief time away from the group, Mitch loses his fear of Curly and they become friends. This is one of their conversations as they head back to the main camp with the strays.

Start Movie: 00:58:42 as the scene opens with a picture of the herd and Mitch says, "And the second its over, she is going to get back into her spaceship and fly away for eternity. Would you do it?"

Stop Movie: 1:01:38 as Mitch looks at his index finger and Curly says, "That's what you gotta figure out."

Approximate Length: 3:14

Questions for Discussion:

1. What did you observe in the conversation? What did you observe in yourself as the scene unfolded?

2. How would you characterize the difference in their outlooks on "choice"?

3. What has value for Curly?

4. Curly says, "You all come up here about the same age, same problems. You spend about fifty weeks a year getting knots in your rope and then you think two weeks up here will untie 'em for ya. None of you get it." To what extent do you think Curly is right? What are some of the knots that get tied in people's ropes in your environment? What are some healthy ways we could avoid letting this process go on without intervention? How do you go about untying the knots?

5. Mitch asks, "What's the one thing?" Curly replies, "That's what you gotta figure out." To what extent have you figured out what "the one thing" is—individually and as a team? Describe it.

Why We Really Like This Clip: Every one of us has priorities in both our professional and private lives. We also have priorities between our personal life and our vocation. We all know people who are workaholics—the job is more important than their own health and family. The consequences of that can be devastating for a person's physical health and the emotional health of the spouse, children, and/or significant others, and it has a profound negative impact on work relationships.

Mitch went on this experience at the same time he was trying to figure out where he is in his own life. His wife supported this trip to help him figure it out since he wasn't much fun to be around. When Curly holds up his finger and says you have to decide on what is most important, Mitch starts to think about his priorities. As a result of this interchange, Mitch starts thinking about all the things in his life and what is most important. At the end of the movie he is clear enough to explain it to his wife and starts taking actions that are congruent with his priorities.

This clip offers an opportunity for individuals and teams to talk about balance. It also affords the chance to talk openly about individual and group goals—what *is* the one (or two or three) thing that is most important?

Notes:

_____

_____

_____

_____

_____

_____

_____

Clip: Bird to Nest

Themes: Courage, persistence, overcoming obstacles, diversity, alternative senses

Film Title & Synopsis: *The Color of Paradise* **(1999).** This Iranian film tells the story of a blind boy, Mohammad. He is a sensitive boy who likes school, learning, and being with people. He is also a well-liked youngster, by his classmates, his sisters, and his grandmother. His father, however, is ashamed of the boy and uneasy around him. As the movie opens, Mohammad waits interminably for his father to pick him up at the end of the school year (everyone else has been gone for hours). His tardy father asks the teacher waiting with Mohammad if there is any way Mohammed could go to school in the summer. The teacher replies that it is impossible. Mohammad and his father head home to the mountains for the summer. Because his father wants to remarry (he is a widower) and does not want to face the complications of having a blind son, he apprentices the boy to a blind carpenter.

Clip Setup: Mohammad is waiting on a park bench for his father to pick him up for the journey back to their home in the mountains at the end of the regular school year. As he waits, he hears the distressed sounds of a small bird that has fallen from its nest. Mohammad reacts by helping the young bird. The scene ends with his father arriving quietly and observing (from a distance) Mohammad washing his hands.

Start Movie: 00:09:46 as Mohammad is sitting on a park bench with his feet on the bench, knees bent so he can rest his head against his knees, while in the distance a man is watering plants. A small bird flies past Mohammad.

Stop Movie: 00:14:25 as Mohammad washes his hands. Unobserved by Mohammad because of his blindness, his father finally arrives and looks disappointedly at Mohammad as Mohammad washes his hands.

Approximate Length: 4:38

Questions for Discussion:

1. What did you observe in yourself and on screen as you watched the clip?

2. What, in your opinion, compelled Mohammad to act?

3. What difficulties did he overcome to replace the bird in the nest? What did you notice about his problem-solving approach?

4. Thinking about your work environment. What things are you now compelled to act on individually, as a team, or as a school?

5. What might we learn from Mohammad about problem solving?

Why We Really Like This Clip: It could have been much easier for Mohammad to simply ignore the little bird's distress. After all, he is blind, so what could he do? Yet he disregarded that course of action and chose to act on his values, even though it would be difficult and might even result in failure or some discomfort to him if he fell, for example. We see this aspect of the clip as a chance to consider acting on values, showing up, going the extra mile, and not making or accepting excuses.

We were also struck by his gentleness in discovering the nature of the problems he faced. He tentatively and sensitively felt for clues in the environment, using the senses he did have to compensate for the one that he did not. While frequently ignored or forgotten in the process of attaining goals, gentleness and sensitivity in going after goals could be the topic of a productive conversation.

Finally, we think that his persistence and his strength are a reminder of the diversity that we require on teams. You might describe his persistence as tentative or soft, yet he continually showed up for the next challenge. Clearly he was able to compensate for his lack of sight. So to build stronger teams and workgroups, we need to remember consistently that not all of us see the world the same way—not all of us have the same abilities in the same areas. Better solutions are more likely from teams with diverse ideas and points of view combined with the persistence to stay the course.

Notes:

_____

_____

_____

_____

_____

_____

_____

_____

Clip: Carpe Diem

Themes: Values, efficacy, perspective, commitment, action

Film Title & Synopsis: *Dead Poets Society* **(1989).** John Keating (Robin Williams) is an out-of-place English teacher in a conservative, all-boys New England prep school. His less-traditional methods and his emphasis on being an individual set him apart from his colleagues but stimulate admiration, interest, and experimentation among the students.

Clip Setup: As the boys get settled for their first class, Mr. Keating walks nonchalantly through the classroom and out of the door, whistling the "1812 Overture." The students sit in stunned silence as he peeks back into the quiet room and says, "Well, come on," inviting them out of the classroom and into the hallway. The boys assemble around a table in front of the trophy case as Keating starts his class with "O Captain, My Captain."

Start Movie: 00:12:16 as the boys gather around a table in the foyer of the classroom building by a trophy case.

Stop Movie: 00:16:35 as Keating, in the midst of the group, whispers loudly, "Carpe, carpe diem. Seize the day, boys. Make your lives extraordinary." Stay with the clip as it captures the looks on the boys' faces and pictures of former students in the trophy case.

Approximate Length: 4:15

Questions for Discussion:

1. What did you observe in the scene? What are your thoughts about "seizing the day"?

2. What is seizing the day? What does it mean for you? For our workgroup?

3. How successful are we (in our workgroup) at seizing the day? How does "seizing the day" get actualized? How might we be better at it?

4. Where do you draw the line between seizing the day and frenetic behavior? Between seizing the day and taking time for reflection?

Why We Really Like This Clip: Mr. Keating surprises the students in his class by not focusing on fact acquisition and conformance to the prescribed curriculum. The students have had many years of doing everything correctly and trying to live up to the standards set by their parents and the prep school. The students are surprised and scared to step out of what they know are the norms and values of the school. Mr. Keating faces the challenge of getting students to think outside of the box or differently from what is expected in the school. Mr. Keating's goal of emotional development as well as cognitive development is countercultural. He does this at considerable risk to himself and creates risk for the students who follow.

Watching the internal struggle of the students as they choose between acting the way they want to and acting in concert with the written rules and expectations of the school is relative to the standards-versus-creativity dichotomy that exists today. We think the answer to this question is both/and. Schools and the United States are struggling with the same issues. Teachers often struggle with this issue on a daily basis. They have to make sure the students have what they need in the short run in terms of knowledge and what they need in the long run like learning to learn, curiosity, creativity, and emotional connections.

We think this clip offers leadership teams, departments, and schools a chance to talk about seizing the day, making the best of things, and being intentional and active about creating a preferred future together. It offers a chance to reflect on how persistent they have been in using their time wisely.

Notes:

_____

_____

_____

_____

_____

_____

_____

_____

Clip: Hubris, Balance

Themes: Hubris, balance, conflicting values, authenticity

Film Title & Synopsis: *Gandhi* **(1982).** The film details the life of Mohandas K. Gandhi (Ben Kingsley), a lawyer who transforms himself and the English colony of India. His emphasis on nonviolent resistance becomes the key as he leads the struggle of the Indian people for independence.

Clip Setup: Gandhi's wife, Kasturb (Rohini Hattangadi), is disturbed because she has to rake and cover the latrines just like everyone else in the ashram. Ever conscious about double standards, Gandhi rejects and belittles his wife, violating his own values and sense of fairness.

Start Movie: 00:22:43 as Gandhi defines *ashram* for *New York Times* reporter Vince Walker (Martin Sheen) and Walker says, "I hear you also participate in preparing the meals and cleaning the toilets. Is that part of the experiment?"

Stop Movie: 00:25:41 when Gandhi's wife says, "And I must rake and cover the latrine."

Approximate Length: 3:00

Questions for Discussion:

1. What did you observe in yourself and the scene as it unfolded?

2. If it is "a matter of principle," how do you resolve situations where different principles are at odds with one another?

3. Thinking about your workplace, what principles seem to matter the most?

4. In your workplace, to what extent are there principles that are at odds or contradictory? How do you, or how can you, resolve the tension created by this situation?

5. Reflecting on your work together as a company, school, team, or department, to what extent does commitment to principle(s) do damage to human relationships? How do you, or how can you, navigate these tricky waters?

6. What advice would you give others who are in this situation?

Why We Really Like This Clip: This clip reminds us of the oft-quoted Rilke passage:

Don't search for the answers, which could not be given to you now, because you would not be able to live them. And the point is, to live everything. Live the questions now. Perhaps then, someday far in the future, you will gradually, without even noticing it, live your way into the answer.

Gandhi has two competing values: We are all equal, so everyone cleans the latrines, but he also feels love and respect for his wife. When values collide, there is perhaps at the moment no answer, no resolution—and the best we can do is live the questions. Persistence cannot be blind obedience to principle or process, but needs to be tempered with thoughtfulness and empathy. This clip reminds us how important it is to talk things out, especially when values are involved.

Having said that, it is clear that persistence is a necessary and positive force for change. It is often the driving engine of change. After all, it was persistence that got the ashram established. So the clip reminds us to be persistent in our goals, not to be possessed by hubris but rather by humility.

Notes:

_____

_____

_____

_____

_____

_____

_____

_____

Clip: Getting the Job

Themes: Commitment, persistence, confidence

Film Title & Synopsis: *Gorillas in the Mist* **(1988).** Based on a true story, the film recounts the work of Dian Fossey (Sigourney Weaver), a physical therapist by trade with no outstanding background or scientific accomplishment, who is moved by her love of animals to volunteer to conduct a census of Rwanda's endangered mountain gorillas. The famous anthropologist Louis Leakey (Iain Cuthbertson) is sponsoring the census. As her work with the gorillas in Africa grows, she discovers and reports publicly that the gorillas are being cruelly ravaged and decimated to the point of extinction for profit. Her obsessive, passionate, and outspoken confrontations lead to her being murdered in 1985, with the killers never being identified.

Clip Setup: Fossey learns that the renowned anthropologist, Dr. Louis Leaky, is giving a public lecture. She has already written to him, but he has not responded. She waits for him outside the lecture hall to propose that she be the one to conduct the census of the mountain gorillas.

Start Movie: 00:03:21 as she smokes outside the lecture hall while it empties.

Stop Movie: 00:05:37 as she is left standing as Dr. Leaky walks away. Hang with the scene as it transitions to the next one—a plane flying, signifying her success with Leaky in getting the job.

Approximate Length: 2:16

Questions for Discussion:

1. What did you observe about Fossey, Leaky, and yourself as the scene progressed?

2. What characteristics of Fossey were particularly effective? How were they effective?

3. What strengths did she bring to the conversation? What drawbacks did you observe?

4. Thinking about your work in your own environment, what is there in this scene that you could keep in mind? What could we learn here? In other words, what is important to remember about questing after our goals? How can we remember these things beyond now—in the long term?

Why We Really Like This Clip: There is a lot to remember about persistence. While our society generally admires the idea of persistence, responses to persistent challenges are often uninspiring and vapid, even hostile. We think it is beneficial to see persistence in action as a reminder of what we must do more often, even at the risk of being annoying and unsettling.

Persistence led Fossey to wait outside the lecture hall for Leakey after having written him a letter. It was that persistence that created an opening for Fossey to introduce herself to Leakey and present her offer. After all, she might have been pushed aside by contributors seeking conversations with Leakey or photographers looking for a photograph. But she would not be deterred.

Beyond that, persistence fueled the energy that led Fossey to think about the arguments she would use with Leakey. Persistence led to preparation and some confidence. And when Leakey asks whether she is up to roughing it in Africa for six months, she answers with a strong, declarative "yes!" When he tries to brush her off by saying he would think about it, she retorts, "How long are you going to think about it? Till all the gorillas are gone?"

It seems to us that persistence is the perfect antidote to counter the toxic internal voices of doubt and despair that arise when one pursues a dream.

Notes:

_____

_____

_____

_____

_____

Clip: Coming Back Again

Themes: Commitment, persistence, values, coming back

Film Title & Synopsis: *Music of the Heart* **(1999).** The film is based on a true story. Roberta Guaspari (Meryl Streep) is a struggling, divorced mother of two who creates an effective music program in East Harlem's troubled school system. The film documents her struggles to create, grow, and keep alive her violin program.

Clip Setup: Roberta is applying for a job to teach music with Principal Janet Williams (Angela Bassett). Devastated but not immobilized by being turned down for lack of experience, Roberta recovers her hope and energy and makes another creative attempt to get a job with Principal Williams.

Start Movie: 00:07:50 as the picture of Central Park East and the address (E. 106th and Madison) come onto the screen.

Stop Movie: 00:12:37 as Roberta backs out of the principal's office saying, "Nice to meet you, Mr. Rausch."

Approximate Length: 4:47

Questions for Discussion:

1. What did you notice in yourself and on screen as you watched the clip?

2. What do you suppose Roberta was thinking and feeling as she continued?

3. What made this work for Roberta?

4. Thinking about your workplace, what attitudes does Roberta exhibit that would help you be more effective and successful individually, as a team, or as an school/district?

5. Focusing on Principal Williams's behavior, what made her an effective leader in this situation?

Why We Really Like This Clip: What we like about this clip is the way persistence interacts with hope, possibility, and an optimistic human spirit. While it looks as if Roberta struck out in her interview with Principal Williams because of lack of experience in inner-city schools and inadequate qualifications, Roberta has other ideas. Persistence motivates! While

Roberta respectfully withdraws from the initial interview, she reappears the following day with a new idea and plenty of outgoing energy. What her persistence brings to the second interview is her confidence in possibility and the hope of success.

The clip is a reminder to us to lighten up a bit, regroup, think creatively, remember the possibilities and the importance of optimism—then to go at it again and again. Like Roberta, we need to keep showing up, keep coming back.

Notes:

_____

_____

_____

_____

_____

_____

_____

Clip: Smitten

Themes: Values, finding yourself/your voice, values, a calling versus a job

Film Title & Synopsis: *October Sky* **(1999).** Based on a true story, the film tells the story of Homer Hickam (Jake Gyllenhaal), a high school student from Coalwood, West Virginia. The time is 1957. Homer, like other boys and their fathers before them, is destined to work in the coal mine. On a wonderfully clear night, however, Homer and a group of neighbors observe *Sputnik* crossing the night sky, and Homer is smitten with the idea of flying rockets. At breakfast the morning after the sighting, Homer announces to his family (mom, dad, and brother) that he is going to fly rockets. And so starts the journey of the real Homer Hickam as he and his three friends, Quentin Wilson (Chris Owen), Roy Lee Cook (William Lee Scott), and Sherman O'Dell (Chad Lindberg), with the support of a teacher, Miss Frieda Riley (Laura Dern), learn to build and fly rockets through trial, error, and correction. Beyond the technical side of learning rocketry, pressures from friends, family, and the community toughen and steel their resolve. Though the film ends as he and his friends win a National Science Award, Homer Hickam goes on to work in NASA's space program.

Clip Setup: On a wonderfully clear night Homer, his friends, and neighbors observe *Sputnik* in the night sky. Homer is smitten with the idea of flying rockets. At breakfast the morning after the sighting, he announces to his family (mom, dad, and brother) that he is going to fly rockets. While his first attempt is a disaster, he is undaunted as he writes to the famous rocket scientist, Werner Von Braun.

Start Movie: 00:07:20 as the teacher asks the class why *Sputnik* is so important. The scene shifts to a group of neighbors looking at the night sky to glimpse *Sputnik*.

Stop Movie: 00:10:49 as the boys look at the destroyed fence. The clip transitions to Homer writing a letter to Werner Von Braun, introducing himself.

Approximate Length: 3:29

Questions for Discussion:

1. What did you observe in yourself and the clip while viewing?

2. How could you tell Homer was smitten?

3. What were the family's reactions to Homer's announcement that he was going to build a rocket? His friends' reactions?

4. What was the result of his attempt to fly a rocket?

5. Thinking about your work together as a company, school, department, or team, what can you learn from this clip about how to approach your projects?

Why We Really Like This Clip: It is important to know that success is not a straight line to glory. The road to success is full of potholes, failures, challenges, and things beyond our control. This clip is about keeping focused on our dream, our goal, even though there are cultural barriers and organizational barriers. We like this because it also shows the importance of teachers in our lives. The teacher was one of the major sources of support for Homer while he pursued his dream. Teachers can open up possibilities, give credibility to our dreams, and provide support for following our passions.

We all need people who support the dreamer in us, those who say, "Hang in there," when it looks bleak. Homer had to face departing from the family expectation of working in the mines to work on something not known to the community or family. Persisting while close relationships are not supporting you is difficult.

Notes:

_____

_____

_____

_____

_____

_____

_____

_____

Clip: Football Practice

Themes: Character, spirit, persistence, commitment, giving it all you have

Film Title & Synopsis: *October Sky* **(1999).** Based on a true story, the film tells the story of Homer Hickam (Jake Gyllenhaal), a high school student from Coalwood, West Virginia. The time is 1957. Homer, like other boys and their fathers before them, is destined to work in the coal mine. On a wonderfully clear night, however, Homer and a group of neighbors observe *Sputnik* crossing the night sky, and Homer is smitten with the idea of flying rockets. At breakfast the morning after the sighting, Homer announces to his family (mom, dad, and brother) that he is going to fly rockets. And so starts the journey of the real Homer Hickam as he and his three friends Quentin Wilson (Chris Owen), Roy Lee Cook (William Lee Scott), and Sherman O'Dell (Chad Lindberg), with the support of a teacher Miss Frieda Riley (Laura Dern) learn to build and fly rockets through trial, error and correction. Beyond the technical side of learning rocketry, pressures from friends, family and the community toughen and steel their resolve. Though the film ends as he and his friends win a National Science Award, Homer Hickam goes on to work in NASA's space program.

Clip Setup: There's not much to do in Coalwood in the mid-1950s. Football (and mining) are the centers of attention in this small West Virginia town. In this clip, Homer is trying out for a place on the football team. The coach puts him into a scrimmage to see what he's got. *Warning:* **This clip contains language that some may find offensive.**

Start Movie: 00:02:06 just after the on-screen title that reads "Based on a true story" as a hand adjusts a radio.

Stop Movie: 00:03:51 as a truck goes by after the boys push the car, complaining that athletes get scholarships and girls.

Approximate Length: 1:45

Questions for Discussion:

1. What did you see? What feelings did the scene evoke?

2. After Homer has been hit a number of times, the coach helps Homer up off the ground and says, "Homer, you sure got guts. But you gotta know when to quit." What is your opinion of that advice? How would you resolve the apparently contradictory advice of Winston Churchill about persistence: "Never, never, never, never give up"?

3. What is the difference between quitting and giving up and changing?

4. As you think about your team, department, school, or district, are there things you should be quitting or giving up on? Describe those. Further, are there areas where you should be changing, which is a kind of giving up?

5. See if you can articulate some of the values or practices that your team, school, or district should never, never, never give up.

Why We Really Like This Clip: Homer shows up for football practice and comes on the field when the coach says, "Let's see what'cha got." Frankly, we like the raw guts that Homer shows on the football field. His persistence brought him to show up with the clear intent of making a mark. We like that determination and persistence and wonder what our schools would be like if more educators felt that way.

We also like the clip because it raises an issue that is important to our work in education—you might be committed to something, you might want something, you might be persistent in going after something, but you "gotta know when to quit." We think that means not quitting, but changing, looking again at what you are doing, rethinking, and reevaluating. Persistence needs to be more than stubbornness—it needs to be commitment with intelligence.

Notes:

_____

_____

_____

_____

_____

_____

_____

Clip: I Quit

Themes: Character, spirit, persistence, commitment, giving it all you have, disappointment

Film Title & Synopsis: *Rudy* **(1993).** Based on a true story, Daniel "Rudy" Ruettiger, Jr. (Sean Astin) has a dream he has nurtured since he was a little boy: He wants to play football for the Fighting Irish of Notre Dame. Rudy and his family live in Joliet, Indiana, where many make their living in the steel mills. Throughout Rudy's life, almost everyone thinks his dream is foolish—his father and brothers, his teachers, his neighbors, and even his girlfriend. Rudy's dad, Daniel (Ned Beatty), wants him to make a career for himself in the steel mills, just as he had done. Others regularly remind Rudy that he is small (as far as football players go), does not have much athletic ability, and is not a very good student. Pete (Christopher Reed), a close friend since high school, seems to be the only one who takes Rudy seriously and doesn't mock his dream.

Rudy graduates from high school. He works in the steel mills while saving his money to attend Notre Dame. After an accident in the factory claims Pete's life, Rudy decides that, having saved a considerable amount of money in the four years since high school, it is time to pursue his dream lest the opportunity pass him by. He boards a bus and begins the journey to playing for Notre Dame.

Clip Setup: Rudy is recognized by many for his character, commitment, and persistence. Rudy has made the practice team and works out regularly with the team, but he is not really good enough to dress with the team for the regular games. Rudy understands that he will never be "great" because of his size and limited talent, yet he does want to experience being on the field with the team at least once—especially for his avid Notre Dame football fan father.

Rudy goes to the coach at the end of his junior year and asks if he could play in at least one game. The coach agrees, but as fortune would have it, the coach quits in the summer and a new one is appointed, not knowing anything of the promise that the previous coach had made.

Rudy continues to play and to hope he will dress for one game. The clip we see here begins with Rudy checking the coach's list to see if he is to suit up for Saturday's game. *Warning:* **This clip contains language that some may find offensive.**

Start Movie: 1:27:57 as Rudy is walking down the hall among students toward the bulletin board with the posted roster for Saturday's game.

Stop Movie: 1:31:41 as Fortune (Charles Dutton), a groundskeeper at the Notre Dame stadium, finishes his talk to Rudy and Rudy looks out as the camera pans the empty stadium.

Approximate Length: 3:45

Questions for Discussion:

1. What in the clip resonated with you?

2. When Rudy bumps into his friend in the hall and tells him he is quitting, he friend gets really mad. Why do you suppose that would happen? How important are dreams and dreamers to other people? What is it that we admire (or hate) about the dreamer?

3. Rudy seems to have reached a breaking point where it seems useless to go on. His response was to quit. What other alternatives did he have?

4. Fortune apparently gives Rudy the support he needs, because Rudy does go to practice. What can you say about Fortune's advice? How would you have advised Rudy and why?

5. Where does persistence like Rudy's come from? In your opinion, does persistence always pay off? Explain. What are the upsides to persistence?

6. Identify and explain places in your team, department, school, or district where persistence is missing. What is the impact on individuals and the school/district? Now identify where persistence is present. What is the impact of that on individuals and the school/district?

Why We Really Like This Clip: In this clip, Rudy has finally decided to give up on his dream. He is angry, depressed, and physically exhausted. At this low point, even with everything Rudy has been through to stay focused, he is ready to quit. Just then, the field groundskeeper talks to him. We think this happens many times in our lives. When things seem dim and despair sets in, a teacher, coach, friend, or sometimes a person we do not know appears to help us rekindle our dream and soul. After the groundskeeper chews him out and gives him the benefit of his own experience, Rudy returns to practice and never looks back.

Notes:

_____

_____

_____

_____

_____

_____

_____

■ FIELD WORK: HOW DOES THIS WORK IN REAL TIME WITH REAL PEOPLE? THE LONELINESS OF A LONG DISTANCE RUNNER

Education Minnesota is the teachers' union for the state. Several years ago, the state NEA (National Education Association) and the AFT (American Federation of Teachers) merged into one organization. At about the same time, consecutive legislatures cut funding to schools and districts for staff development, either outright or by creating alternative loopholes for designated staff development monies.

In response, Education Minnesota, with grants from both the NEA and the AFT, developed a training program for local Professional Development Activists (PDAs), the theory being somewhat Peace Corp–like—train and develop local leaders to organize school cultures around the concept of learning communities. Clearly this is difficult, long-term work that requires commitment and a steady hand.

The issue of persistence came up. In the face of overwhelming challenges, nay-sayers, legislative financial abandonment, changing personnel, and doing the hard, exhausting work of teaching, it is understandable that PDAs get down at times and want to give up.

To recapture some of the verve, to rejuvenate or rekindle, to give direction once more, our training team, which included some of the gifted members of the Education Minnesota staff, decided to include the idea of efficacy in our training.

We were training a group of about 75 PDAs in a large room with round tables seating six to eight per table. We had identified about 10 quotes relating to persistence and put each quote on one sheet of 8.5 × 11 paper. Fearing that the quotes would be too difficult to read, we went to Kinkos and had the quotes enlarged so they could be taped to the walls around the room and easily read by the participants.

As a preliminary exercise, after people introduced themselves at their tables, the participants were to circulate around the room, reading the quotations posted on the walls. After they read them all, they were to go stand by the one that really resonated with them. Some quotations had large groups around them, so the group had to be split with the same assignment: Talk to the others in your group about what this quote says to you and why you find it important. What would you want to tell others about this quote? After about 10 minutes, we went around the room, asking for reports from the group about the substance of their conversations.

We then reconvened as a large group. We told the participants that we were going to view a film clip that we thought had a lot to do with persistence. To set up the clip, we told them about the movie—the general story, the scene, the characters. Then we told them, in general, what they would be seeing, that is, in this scene John Keating (Robin Williams) is teaching an important lesson about seizing the day. We asked them to observe not only what was going on in the clip, but to be aware of what was going on within themselves as the scene unfolded. Having cued up the tape to where we wanted to begin, we then showed the clip. As it was a large group in a large room, we showed it through a LCD projector and, as we did not have large speakers, propped the microphone we were using next to the speaker so everyone could hear.

After the clip was finished, each table was instructed to look for the half-sheet of paper with guiding discussion questions on their table. There were enough for all to have a copy of the questions. For 15 minutes or so, they worked their way through the questions. At the conclusion, we asked for volunteers to report on the substance of their discussions. Alternatively, we could have focused on one question (e.g., what does it mean for a teacher or school to seize the day?) and asked for comments related to the one question.

We had identified and reproduced a 1.5-page piece on efficacy (Costa & Garmston, 1994, pp. 133–135) we wanted them to engage. We passed it out. We said we were having a 20-minute break to refill coffee, snacks, and so on, and that we wanted them to read the short piece as well during the break.

When we reconvened as a large group after the break, the groups were instructed to organize around an activity to process the article. We were making the case for renewed efficacy and persistence, even in the face of daunting challenges.

IN OTHER WORDS: QUOTES FOR ■ EXTENDING THINKING AND CONVERSATIONS

One may go a long way after one is tired.

—French Proverb

Fall seven times, stand up eight.

—Japanese Proverb

Do not seek to follow in the footsteps of the men of old; seek what they sought.

—Matsuo Basho

Not to know is bad; not to wish to know is worse.

—African Proverb

Everyone has talent. What is rare is the courage to follow the talent to the dark place where it leads.

—Erica Jong

Success is getting up one more time than getting knocked down.

—Eleanor Roosevelt

Of all the things I've done, the most vital is coordinating those who work with me and aiming their efforts at a certain goal.

—Walt Disney

You may have to fight a battle more than once to win it.

—Margaret Thatcher

One's work may be finished some day, but one's education never.

—Alexandre Dumas

Rather than considering whether you're making a difference, remember—you are the difference.

—Sandy McDaniels

Studies indicate that the one quality all successful people have is persistence. They're willing to spend more time accomplishing a task and to persevere in the face of many difficult odds. There's a very positive relationship between people's ability to accomplish any task and the time they're willing to spend on it.

—Joyce Brothers

I will persist until I succeed. Always will I take another step. If that is of no avail I will take another, and yet another. In truth, one step at a time is not too difficult . . . I know that small attempts, repeated, will complete any undertaking.

—Og Mandino

Persistence is what makes the impossible possible, the possible likely, and the likely definite.

—Robert Half

I am not judged by the number of times I fail, but by the number of times I succeed. And the number of times I succeed is in direct proportion to the number of times I can fail and keep trying.

—Tom Hopkins

Nothing in the world can take the place of persistence. Talent will not; nothing is more common than unsuccessful men with talent. Genius will not; unrewarded genius is almost a proverb. Education will not; the world is full of educated derelicts. Persistence and determination alone are omnipotent.

—Calvin Coolidge

A basic truth of management—if not of life—is that nearly everything looks like a failure in the middle . . . persistent, consistent execution is unglamorous, time-consuming, and sometimes boring.

—Rosabeth Moss Kanter

Do all the good you can,
By all the means you can,
In all the ways you can,
In all the places you can,
At all the times you can,
To all the people you can,
As long as ever you can.

—John Wesley

Spectacular achievements are always preceded by unspectacular preparation.

—Roger Staubach

We must not, in trying to think about how we can make a big difference, ignore the small daily differences we can make which, over time, add up to big differences that we often cannot foresee.

—Marian Wright Edelman

Money grows on the tree of persistence.

—Japanese Proverb

To be nobody-but-yourself—in a world which is doing its best, night and day, to make you everybody else—means to fight the hardest battle which any human being can fight; and never stop fighting.

—e. e. cummings

When one door closes another one opens; but we so often look so long and so regretfully upon the closed door, that we do not see the ones which open for us.

—Alexander Graham Bell

Do not confuse motion and progress. A rocking horse keeps moving but does not make any progress.

—Alfred A. Montapert

One person with a belief is equal to a force of ninety-nine who have only interests.

—John Stuart Mill

All greatness is improbable; what's probable is tedious and petty.

—Lao Tzu

Talk doesn't cook the rice.

—Chinese proverb

Children need models more than critics.

—French proverb

■ ARTICLES FOR STUDY CIRCLES

DuFour, R. (2004). What is a "professional learning community"? *Educational Leadership, 61*(8), 6–11.

Hargreaves, A., & Fink, D. (2004). The seven principles of sustainable leadership. *Educational Leadership, 61*(7), 8–13.

Patterson, D., & Rolheiser, C. (2004). Creating a culture of change: Ten strategies for developing an ethic of teamwork. *Journal of Staff Development, 25*(2), 1–4.

Peterson, K. D. (2002). Positive or negative? *Journal of Staff Development, 23*(3), 10–15.

Posner, D. (2004). What's wrong with teaching to the test? *Phi Delta Kappan, 85*(10), 749–751.

Richardson, J. (2000, August-September). Smart moves: Achieving your vision depends on follow-through. *Tools for Schools* [available at http://nsdc.org/library/publications/tools/tools9-00rich.cfm].

Saphier, J., & King, M. (1985). Good seeds grow in strong cultures. *Educational Leadership, 42*(6), 67–74.

■ BOOKS FOR EXTENDED LEARNING

Bennis, W. (1997). *Managing people is like herding cats.* Provo, UT: Executive Excellence Publishing.

Carse, J. P. (1986). *Finite and infinite games.* New York: Ballantine..

Collins, J. (2001). *Good to great.* New York: HarperCollins.

Costa, A., & Kallick, B. (2002). *Habits of mind.* Alexandria, VA: ASCD.

Costa, A. L., & Garmston, R. J. (1994). *Cognitive coaching: A foundation for renaissance schools.* Norwood, MA: Christopher-Gorden Publishers.

Covey, S. R. (1989). *The 7 habits of highly effective people.* New York: Simon & Schuster.

Freedman, D. H. (2000). *Corps business.* New York: HarperCollins.

Garfield, C. (1986). *Peak performers.* New York: Avon.

Leonard, G. (1991*). Mastery.* New York: Plume.

Tzu, S. (1963). *The art of war* (S. B. Griffith, Trans.). Oxford, UK: Oxford University Press.

Film Clips That Explore Creativity and Building Capacity

4

It's like driving a car at night. You never see further than your headlights, but you can make the whole trip that way.

—E. L. Doctorow

Einstein said, "You can't solve problems with the same kind of thinking that got you into them." We have used this quote in workshops for many years. In the final analysis, if what you are doing is not working, then try something else. This may be the simplest answer to a complex problem.

Usually, if something is not working, we try harder, we say the same thing over and over again hoping for different results, and/or we try to convince others that we are right. The opening line of Robert Pascale's book, *Managing on the Edge*, says, "Nothing fails like success." Think about it. If your way has always worked, why would you try something else? Most of us dig in and stay the course. Unfortunately, in times of turmoil and high change, that might be the worst thing to do. The same can be said for businesses and schools as well.

Edward de Bono, an expert on creativity, said years ago that creativity will be our most important advantage. Dr. Art Costa has advocated for years to keep flexibility in thinking and creativity in schools. If you read the business literature for the past several years, you will see increasing numbers of articles about creativity and innovation as lifeblood for organizations. There are books on intellectual capital, two with this very same title. Andy Hargreaves is the first educator we know of who has actively written about the knowledge economy, what is coming in the future, and what we need in schools to prepare young people for a very different world than most adults know now.

Adults' frame of reference is what they experienced. Most adults know what school is like from when they attended as children. Unfortunately, our children, and all students today, live in a different time with different skills needed for success. We are preparing our students for a world which we know very little about. This can keep us up at night. How do we prepare students for their future instead of a world that will no longer exist?

In Tom Stewart's (1997) book, *Intellectual Capital,* he makes the argument that businesses and organizations need this as a mainstay to solve problems. The people who will be working in those companies will be coming from schools that either prepare young people or do not. Stewart says we need three things for this. First, we need human capital. How do we prepare students to work in industries that have not been created yet? Second, we need structural capital. How do we build and organize schools or companies with the infrastructure to support and generate intellectual capital? Third, we need customer capital. How do we get and use feedback from our customers to initiate, create, and develop new ideas?

In 10 years of doing workshops, we have asked all kinds of audiences what they are looking for from the high school graduates, college graduates, and nongraduates they want to hire. The answer is consistently two things, in this order: First, can the person work on a diverse team? There are not many jobs where interacting as teams is not the norm. Second, can they think creatively? We do not need more people who think the same; we need people who look at the same information and see something different.

Michael G. Zey, in his book *Seizing the Future,* states that there are plans to colonize the moon by 2010 and Mars by 2019. Japan has plans to build an underground city to hold 500,000 people and to construct an island to hold 1,000,000 people. Plans exist for the greening of the Sahara Desert to grow food, for magnetic-levitation transportation systems that travel 400 miles per hour, and for machines that would be injected into our bloodstream to eat cholesterol. Our question is, "How are we preparing students to work in these industries?" Learning to learn will be even more important to students as they go from career to career. People will have intellectual capital as a resource to sell to employers.

A problem occurs to those of us who are writing this. How do businesses and schools organize to produce the kind of talent that will be required for the future? Businesses have a head start, which will always be the case. Schools will be required to develop people with needed skills and intellectual capacity or businesses will have to find them elsewhere.

The following clips, quotes, questions, and activities are designed to stretch our thinking and create dialogue to develop the intellectual capital in our organizations. Three strong suggestions are

1. Read *Re-Imagine* by Tom Peters.

2. Read *Whoever Makes the Most Mistakes Wins* by Richard Farson.

3. Practice improvisational skills. Start by going to stevie@stevierays.com.

CLIPS ■

Clip: Forget the Plan

Themes: Improvisation, creativity, thinking creatively, reframing, reaching decisions

Film Title & Synopsis: *Apollo 13* **(1995).** Astronauts Jim Lovell (Tom Hanks), Fred Haise (Bill Paxton), and Jack Swigert (Kevin Bacon) and a ground crew led by Ken Mattingly (Gary Sinise) and Gene Kranz (Ed Harris) struggle to save the crew on a crippled space ship that is 205,000 miles from earth on its way to the moon in 1970. An explosion on board has crippled the mother ship. They must figure out a way to stay alive and return to earth with only the dwindling resources onboard.

Clip Setup: Reacting to the disaster that has struck the crippled space ship and the possibility of losing the crew, Gene Kranz begins to organize his team to improvise a plan to "get our people home."

Start Movie: 1:07:05 as Kranz enters the room for a meeting and says, "OK, people, listen up. I want you all to forget the flight plan."

Stop Movie: 1:09:08 as the words "Day 4" come onto the middle of the screen.

Approximate Length: 2:02

Questions for Discussion:

1. What did you see? What were the significant moments?

2. How did they arrive at a decision? What were the most important steps in reaching the conclusion that they would "slingshot" the capsule around the moon?

3. Both listening and summarizing seemed important in the process. What was the impact of each on the process?

4. How were divergent views dealt with?

5. Assess and talk about how effective you are in your team/department/school/organization with respect to listening, summarizing, and dealing with divergent views and reaching decisions.

Why We Really Like This Clip: Sometimes plans are very important for long-term goals, lesson plans for a successful class, and personal growth plans for you. When most of us were 18, we knew all the answers. Since that time, as we have lived life, we have realized there are not many right answers. There are many answers, and we must choose between the possibilities. Gene Kranz had to shift the ground crew's thinking from working the plan to reacting to midcourse problems.

Think about how many times the plan you started with did not work or at least had some gaps in the implementation. We think running organizations, schools and classrooms, and teams is becoming more improvisational. Success is meeting those problems, finding a new pathway, and getting into action that will make the project a success. Gene Kranz had to create new thinking based on the problems that were presented at that moment. He had to do this even though some people were wedded to their previous plan and some were even emotionally attached to their plan.

The clip offers teams and organizations a chance to reflect on and evaluate their own creativity in dealing with challenges, developing new approaches, and responding to unforeseen problems.

Notes:

_____

_____

_____

_____

_____

_____

_____

_____

Clip: Standing on the Desk

Themes: Reframe, perspective, looking again, change

Film Title & Synopsis: *Dead Poets Society* **(1989).** John Keating (Robin Williams) is an out-of-place English teacher in a conservative, New England all-boys prep school. His less-traditional practice and his emphasis on being an individual set him apart from his colleagues but stimulate admiration, interest, and experimentation among the students.

Clip Setup: In the midst of having a discussion in class, Keating hops up on his desk and continues the talk. He asks some serious questions about perspective, questioning, and striking out on one's own.

Start Movie: 00:42:48 as Keating hops up onto his desk and says, "Why do I stand up here?"

Stop Movie: 00:44:35 as Keating leaves the classroom, then ducks back in and says, "Mr. Anderson, don't think I don't know that this assignment scares the hell out of you, you mole." Keating then turns off the lights.

Approximate Length: 1:46

Questions for Discussion:

1. What struck you in the scene? Why?

2. To what extent do you agree with Keating when he says, "We must constantly look at things in a different way."

3. Keating invites the boys to stand on his desk to show them that "the world looks very different from up here." Reflecting on your work environment, how (besides standing on your desk) could you experience things looking differently? What impact would that (seeing things from different perspectives) have on your work together as a team or group?

4. "Just when you think you know something, you have to look at it in another way. Even though it may seem silly or wrong, you must try!" Reflect on your work environment and see if you can identify things that you are certain of that you may have to look at another way. Explain your thinking.

5. How do you resolve the tension of being a team player while still finding "your own voice"?

6. Think of yourself, your team or department, or your organization. What are some ways you could broaden your perspectives? What might the impact of a broadened perspective be?

Why We Really Like This Clip: Looking at a problem longer or harder for a solution generally does not work. If something is not working, try something else. Charles Garfield (1986), in his book *Peak Performers*, says that stars know when to press on and when to abandon their plan. Einstein said, "Insanity is continuing to do the same thing and expecting different results." To find another way to solve problems, it can help to look at the problem from a new perspective.

We think that is what this clip demonstrates. Take another look, look from another angle, and see the issues from another point of view—are all lessons to be gleaned from this clip. We also think you can use this clip to help people understand the risk of thinking outside the box or with a creative mind-set. Adults and students need to understand that being creative can involve risk. Teachers and administrators must learn the same lesson. How do you create safety when thinking creatively?

Notes:

_____

_____

_____

_____

_____

_____

_____

_____

Clip: Explaining the Plan

Themes: Leadership, dealing with divergent ideas, encouragement, creative thinking, implementing ideas

Film Title & Synopsis: *Flight of the Phoenix* **(1965).** A plane piloted by Frank Towns (James Stewart) crashes in a sandstorm in the Sahara Desert. The situation is hopeless—men are injured or have died, there are fights among the men, water is scarce, it is too far to walk out, there is excruciating heat in the day and bone-chilling cold at night, and rescue is unlikely because the plane was way off course due to instrument malfunction. One of the dozen or so men onboard who survives the crash is Heinrich Dorfmann (Hardy Krüger), an airplane designer who calculates that it would be possible to use the undamaged wing of the downed plane to construct another airplane to fly the survivors out of the desert. The film is about their struggle to work together to complete the task.

Clip Setup: Heinrich Dorfmann and Frank Towns, the pilot of the downed aircraft, have already had a heated exchange about Dorfmann's idea to rebuild the plane. Lew Moran (Richard Attenborough) finds out that Dorfmann is an aircraft designer and wants Towns to talk with Dorfmann further.

Start Movie: 00:55:20 as, in the dark cabin of the plane, Towns says to Moran, "Alright, I'll talk to him, Lew. If it makes you happy, I'll talk to him." The scene immediately shifts to Dorfmann standing outside and looking down at his plans; he says, "There's no component problem. The port boom is undamaged and. . . ."

Stop Movie: 1:01:16 as Dorfmann says to Towns, "The only thing outstanding about you, Mr. Towns, is your stupidity." Dorfmann turns and walks away and Moran restrains Towns from going after him.

Approximate Length: 6:00

Questions for Discussion:

1. What did you observe? What were the underlying dynamics of the situation?

2. What are the problems being voiced by others about the challenging plan?

3. To what extent was this a productive exchange? What is the basis for your judgment?

4. What exact language did Towns use that exacerbated the situation?

5. How would you describe Dorfmann's attitude and conduct in his interaction with Towns? Similarly, how would you describe Towns's attitude and conduct with respect to Dorfmann?

6. What behavior might have made this a more productive "meeting"?

7. You might say that Towns was making excuses, appealing to the weaknesses of the group, defending the status quo, while Dorfmann was pointing to possibilities and challenges. You might also view Towns as being realistic and Dorfmann as unrealistic. Who is more appropriate and why? What side would you have been on in this debate? Why?

8. How is this scene a story that is repeated over and over again in organizations? See if you can articulate any insights you have about your own organization (school, department, team) relative to this clip. How might this apply to your situation?

Why We Really Like This Clip: We like several features about this clip. First, Towns's reaction to Dorfmann's ideas are classic—new ideas frequently suffer the harsh derision of other people, from people who should know better. You would think that, given the grave situation, any idea would be appreciated and explored for its merits.

Another reason we like this clip is that it shows creativity at its best—thinking beyond the situation, outside normal definitions—to come up with a unique way to solve a problem. While many of the problems presented required thought, planning, consideration, and energy, none seemed as big as attitude, pessimism, and being stuck in the desert.

Finally, we think the clip introduces the idea that there may be underlying principles at work despite the size of the "plane." What principles, for example, buttress successful organizations, whether in a school or General Motors? What factors tend to create toxic work cultures, whether in a district office or a production line? The clip offers an opportunity to consider a larger picture, one that might lead to "systems thinking," that is, systemwide conversations, planning, and reflecting for action.

Notes:

_____

_____

_____

_____

_____

_____

_____

_____

Clip: All Hell Breaks Loose

Themes: Planting resources or ideas in an environment, unintended consequences

Film Title & Synopsis: *Ice Age* (2002). Set in the Ice Age, this is an animated story of four characters (Sid the sloth, Manny the mammoth, Diego the saber-toothed tiger, and Scrat the saber-toothed, squirrel-like creature) who are migrating south with all the other animals for warmer climes. A human baby is discovered, the survivor of an attack by tigers on a human camp. Trying to escape the tigers, a mother (baby in her arms) jumped into a swollen river and was lost. The baby has washed up on shore. Except for Diego, who wants to return the baby to the tigers, the other animal characters decide that they will find the father and return the baby to him.

Clip Setup: In this scene, Scrat is attempting to bury his acorn in the snow. He keeps forcing it, only to discover that it cracks the glacier in a massive and fundamental way. He barely escapes, surviving a long fall only to be hit on the head by the acorn and stepped on by a mammoth.

Start Movie: 00:00:00 as a creature (Scrat) is hopping along in a snowy environment, grasping an acorn. He is attempting to find a place to bury it.

Stop Movie: 00:03:09 as Scrat lands after a long fall and is immediately stepped on by a wooly mammoth. The acorn follows, hitting Scrat on the head.

Approximate Length: 3:09

Questions for Discussion:

1. What do you see? What reactions did you experience as you watched the clip?

2. If we think of this as an allegory or fable about work life or organizations, what might the acorn represent? Scrat? The glacier and other features of the environment? The mammoth's foot?

3. How might you interpret the story as it relates to real life in a school or organization?

4. To what extent does it parallel your experience in your work environment when ideas are forced? Be specific.

5. What other strategies, besides force, might be used to accomplish the task(s)?

6. What are some things, personally and organizationally, that you are not willing to let go of—like the acorn? What is the impact of not letting go of those things on people, performance, and the organization?

Why We Really Like This Clip: We like this clip because it offers an opportunity to be creative about organizational issues. We see this as a story, a warning really, about what can happen when any person or group tries to force his ideas or values (acorn) into the environment. In this case, a huge crack in a glacier occurs, sending Scrat running for his life as the glacier shifts—but not without his acorn. As a matter of fact, he holds on to his acorn (ideas and values?) through his descent from the glacier. When Scrat finally lands, followed by his beloved acorn hitting him on the head, the wooly mammoth might be seen as the bureaucracy stepping on him, further punishing him for his bureaucratic indiscretion. We think that groups can have some fun talking about the symbols in this clip and gain some insight into the dynamics of their own organization.

Notes:

_____

_____

_____

_____

_____

_____

_____

_____

Clip: The Final Interview

Themes: Flow, values, multiple intelligences

Film Title & Synopsis: *Billy Elliot* **(2000).** Eleven-year-old Billy Elliot (Jamie Bell) rejects boxing lessons at the gym and quite accidentally discovers a love and talent for dance. He struggles with his father (Gary Lewis) and brother (Jamie Draven) (both of whom are involved in an ugly miners' strike), who ridicule Billy's love of dance.

Clip Setup: Billy had a good audition at the Royal Ballet School but got into a fight with another student while waiting for the final interview. As the scene opens, the chair of the committee is saying that violence cannot be condoned and that the fight would be considered as they reach a final decision on whether to admit Billy. Just as he is leaving after a disastrous interview, Billy is asked one last question. A sympathetic interviewer, sensing the impending doom, says, "Just one last question. Can I ask you, Billy, what does it feel like when you are dancing?"

Start Movie: 1:26:20 as Billy and his dad sit on chairs in a large, empty room.

Stop Movie: 1:30:28 as Billy walks down the stairs, followed by his dad with suitcase in hand, and out the door of the Royal Academy.

Approximate Length: 3:24

Questions for Discussion:

1. As you observed this scene, what were your thoughts and feelings?

2. What are some of the images Billy uses to describe himself dancing and the feelings he has when dancing?

3. To what extent do you think such flow is needed to pursue a craft, art, or profession? Your work?

4. In your opinion, how does one develop the ability to experience "electricity" or "flying"?

5. Under what circumstances have you felt this way?

6. In your opinion, is it possible to feel this way about and at work in your school or organization? Explain. What contributes to and militates against cultivating this state in your environment?

7. What impact does being able to achieve the "electric" or "flying" state have on the individual and the organization?

Why We Really Like This Clip: So often it is hard to get in touch with one's own creativity. There is usually so much to do and not much support for cultivating creativity in organizations.. How do you touch it, ignite it, tap into it? In a way, that is what happened to Billy when he was asked to describe what it is like when he dances. He was stunned, without easy words. It is a marvelous example of what a good coach can do. As Billy quietly started to explore and articulate the sensation of dancing, it became clear that he had a special connection to dance. We really liked the quiet and stillness of Billy as he described what it is like to be "in the zone." His reflective practice before our eyes reminds us of the importance of taking time to reflect and articulate our deepest experiences. To us, discussions and explanations of this sort are virtually absent from our conversations with one another in schools and in most organizations. The clip reinforces the necessity that we take time to frame and answer questions like this and in this manner in our work from time to time. It also makes us wonder how much better organizations and schools would be if we could do this for each other—coaching each other to deeper levels of reflection.

Notes:

_____

_____

_____

_____

_____

_____

_____

Clip: Coaching

Themes: Coaching, creation, poetry, focus

Film Title & Synopsis: *Dead Poets Society* **(1989).** John Keating (Robin Williams) is an out-of-place English teacher in a conservative, New England all-boys prep school. His less-traditional practice and his emphasis on being an individual set him apart from his colleagues but stimulate admiration, interest, and experimentation among the students.

Clip Setup: Keating gave the assignment of writing a poem to be read aloud in class. After listening to and commenting on the poetry of two students, he calls on Todd Anderson (Ethan Hawke), who admits he did not do his assignment. Keating seems determined to make something successful happen here for the boy and guides him through a creative process in real time.

Start Movie: 00:54:58 as, after advising a student, "Just don't let your poems be ordinary," Mr. Keating walks through the classroom searching for the next student to read his poem. He stops in front of a student's desk, points, and says, "Now who's next? Mr. Anderson? You're sitting there in agony!"

Stop Movie: 00:57:51 as the class is clapping for the spontaneous poetry Todd Anderson has recited, Keating whispers into the boy's ear, "Don't you forget this!"

Approximate Length: 3:53

Questions for Discussion:

1. What were your reactions to the clip?

2. If you had to describe the creative process as seen here, what elements are necessary?

3. How would you describe your own creative process? And that of your work group or organization?

4. To what extent is the creative process the same for groups as for individuals?

5. What cultivates the creativity of groups? Of individuals?

6. What depresses our ability as groups and individuals to be creative?

7. Thinking of your work group/department/team/organization. Assess and describe the extent of your creativity. What cultivates and what inhibits creativity in your work environment? Describe areas of work that require more creativity.

Why We Really Like This Clip: We like the idea that Todd's intellectual creativity was related to his physical being. Keating knew this and asked Todd to stand and get into a "yawping stance"—"you can't yawp sitting down." ("Yawping" means uttering a sharp cry.) Todd needed that physical involvement to finally and forcefully yawp. There was movement as well. It is as if Keating used movement to keep Todd off balance and confused, so his usual responses and words were lost or hidden from him. Not having the usual responses available to him, he had to create new ones. Further, Keating has Todd close his eyes, thereby not allowing him to focus on his surroundings, but instead sending him into his mind and making him conscious. Even when Todd opens his eyes in response to the rest of the class laughing at his creative words, Keating covers his eyes and tells him to close them again. The clip makes us wonder if doing more physical things together (such as improvisational exercises or simply walking as we search for answers) could increase our creativity.

We also liked the invitation that Keating issued to Todd to simply start talking, to start describing the picture of Walt Whitman. Keating continually challenges Todd, thereby forcing him deeper into his creative expressions. It was a game they were both voluntarily playing, although Todd seemed more reluctant and hesitant. Keating continually gave support and positive feedback as they delved deeper into Todd's creative expression. The clip could open a discussion about the extent we think or talk about things versus the idea of "just do it." A team or organization might also examine how much support and feedback exist for creative endeavors.

Notes:

Clip: Model Planes

Themes: Creativity, communication, questioning, underlying principles

Film Title & Synopsis: *Flight of the Phoenix* **(1965).** A plane piloted by Frank Towns (James Stewart) crashes in a sandstorm in the Sahara Desert. The situation is hopeless—men are injured or have died, fights are breaking out among the men, water is scarce, it is too far to walk out, there is excruciating heat in the day and shivering cold at night, and rescue is unlikely because the plane was way off course due to instrument malfunction. One of the dozen or so men on board who survives the crash is Heinrich Dorfmann (Hardy Krüger), an airplane designer who calculates that it would be possible to use the undamaged wing of the downed plane to construct another airplane to fly them out of the desert. The film is about their struggle to work together to complete the task.

Clip Setup: The impossible has almost been completed—the men are finishing the construction of an aircraft made from the wreckage as conceived, planned, and directed by the aircraft designer, Heinrich Dorfmann. The work has been grueling and exhausting. One more surprise is revealed in this clip—Dorfmann, in a casual conversation with the pilot, Frank Towns, and Lew Moran (Richard Attenborough), reveals that he designs model airplanes, not "the real thing."

Start Movie: 1:56:03 with a quick shot of the sun rising behind the newly constructed airplane. Immediately the scene moves to inside the living quarters. Towns and Moran are approaching Dorfmann as Moran says, "The fairings are about ready but you'll need to look at the controlling."

Stop Movie: 2:01:52 at the campfire, with the camera moving toward Moran, who is leaning his head against the doorframe of the living quarters, simultaneously laughing and crying almost hysterically.

Approximate Length: 5:49

Questions for Discussion:

1. What did you see in this clip? What did you find interesting or intriguing?

2. As cited by Moran, Dorfmann really does not think that there is any difference between designing model planes and full-sized airplanes. The principles are the same, though you might encounter different problems. To what extent do you think that is true of organizations—that there are fundamental principles upon which successful teams or organizations are built?

3. What are the underlying principles of a successful team or organization? Why are the principles important to the success of the enterprise?

4. How can a team or organization cultivate the important principles named above?

Why We Really Like This Clip: There are several features that we find compelling in this clip. The clip seems to suggest that there are principles that apply to small and large aircraft equally. It is those common principles that Dorfmann uses to calculate and assemble the new airplane. We, too, think there are key principles in organizations that produce success such as, but not limited to, the development of trust, shared visions and goals, broad staff participation, and commitment. We think these principles apply to nonprofits as well as for-profits, huge organizations and small ones, whether producing widgets or educating children.

Another feature about the clip is the lack of completeness in the talking and planning that went into the project. Why, for example, are they just finding out the truth about Dorfmann's designing experience as the project is being completed—when they are almost ready to take off in the redesigned and reconstructed plane? It reminds us of the importance of taking time to have thorough, thoughtful conversations about important matters. On the contrary, the agenda or "to do" list is usually long and normally inhibits deep, quality conversations. That is why it must be a priority to organize time, schedules, and personnel to have efficient meetings that matter on a regular basis. As Goethe said, "Things that matter most must never be at the mercy of things that matter least."

Finally, how utterly fascinating that Dorfmann saw the underlying principles of flight and could make the creative leap from designing small aircraft (model airplanes) to "the real thing," as Towns calls it. It makes us wonder what small, unnoticed principles we miss that might shed light on some of our most complicated problems. Our task, then, is to be fully present and open to new ideas and approaches. Thinking more widely and looking for similarities might well lead us to some interesting analyses and solutions.

Notes:

_____

_____

_____

_____

_____

_____

_____

FIELD WORK: HOW DOES THIS WORK IN REAL TIME WITH REAL PEOPLE? OTHER PEOPLE'S MONEY

Once, a few years ago, there was a middle-aged school superintendent from the Midwest who was wise beyond his years. He faced a familiar story: The legislature was reducing funding, so the district was faced with a multimillion-dollar cut that needed to be made for the following year. It was the middle of March, always the toughest time of the school year, and he knew he needed to start thinking and planning for the enormous decisions that would have to be made.

He knew that the success of the organization depended on team work and meeting challenges as a team. He had been carefully planting the seeds that would help the district grow into a learning organization. However, all of that seemed threatened now because, in times of scarcity and difficulty, relationships sour, competition and secrecy become the norm, and progressive, productive work grinds to a halt while everyone tries to protect what is theirs.

Because he was an optimist and a deep and broad thinker, he decided to call together key leaders from the district—union leaders, all department heads, all of his cabinet. His goal was for all of them to wrestle with the problem up front and openly, ahead of the coming crisis. While the group numbered about 60, the seriousness of the situation and the fact all were at the table lent an air of quiet openness to the room.

After reporting what the status of the legislative action was, he went on to say that we needed to decide how we were going to proceed, how we were going to make the cuts to cover the projected deficit. He said that it was important that we all talk honestly and respectfully with one another. As we were in a cafeteria, we were seated at tables in groups of six to eight. On each table were pink sheets with quotations about creativity on them—all of the sheets were the same, so each person at the table had their own copy. We were to introduce ourselves, tell what we did in the district, and pick a quote we admired and say why we thought it was great. In a short while the superintendent reconvened the large group.

Because of the looming crisis, the superintendent opined, we would be required to think in different ways if we were to manage the difficulty successfully. He had us watch a clip from *Dead Poet's Society*, where John Keating (Robin Williams) hops up onto the teacher's desk and continues to lecture the class about seeing things from a different perspective.

When the clip was over we talked in groups (a guided discussion) about how important it was in our current situation to see things differently, from a different perspective. Besides jumping on desks, we were asked to think about how we could broaden our perspectives and how valuable it would be in helping us make wise decisions. So everyone felt that their work and views were important, and each group reported on the nature of their discussion.

We spent the rest of the meeting drawing up our agenda for the next two months' work. He sent us home with an article, Robert J. Garmston's "Graceful Conflict," and said we would be talking about it in groups of six to eight people at our next meeting. As we enjoyed the film clip and our chance to talk to one another about it, we were happy to hear him intimate that we may see another clip at the next meeting.

After the meeting ended, curious about his use of media in this way, I asked the superintendent where he got the idea for the clip.

He said, "I was always impressed with that movie, and I have two or three favorite scenes. It just struck me that it would be an interesting way to communicate what I deeply believe—that we are in a situation that requires thinking differently, from the perspective of the whole, not the turf I control. I arranged with the audio-visual department to have a VCR, a large screen, an LCD projector, and speakers so I could simply pop in my copy of the videotape I bought years ago 'cause I like the film so much. Last night, I simply fast-forwarded the tape to the place I wanted to start at, as I knew what I was looking for. And I put it in this morning."

■ IN OTHER WORDS: QUOTES FOR EXTENDING THINKING AND CONVERSATIONS

The intuitive mind is a sacred gift and the rational mind is a faithful servant. We have created a society that honors the servant and has forgotten the gift.

—Albert Einstein

There is nothing in a caterpillar that tells you it's going to be a butterfly.

—Buckminster Fuller

Creativity requires the courage to let go of certainties.

—Erich Fromm

The best way to have a good idea is to have lots of ideas.

—Linus Pauling

You need chaos in your soul to give birth to a dancing star.

—Nietzsche

Creativity is a central source of meaning in our lives . . . [and] when we are involved in it, we feel that we are living more fully than during the rest of life.

—Mihaly Csikszentmihalyi

Creativity is not the finding of a thing, but the making something out of it after it is found.

—James Russell Lowell

Creativity is allowing oneself to make mistakes; art is knowing which ones to keep.

—Scott Adams

Creativity arises out of the tension between spontaneity and limitations, the latter (like the river banks) forcing the spontaneity into the various forms which are essential to the work of art or poem.

—Rollo May

While we have the gift of life, it seems to me the only tragedy is to allow part of us to die whether it is our spirit, our creativity or our glorious uniqueness.

—Gilda Radner

There are painters who transform the sun to a yellow spot, but there are others who with the help of their art and their intelligence, transform a yellow spot into the sun.

—Pablo Picasso

I'm always thinking about creating. My future starts when I wake up every morning . . . Every day I find something creative to do with my life.

—Miles Davis

Why should we all use our creative power? Because there is nothing that makes people so generous, joyful, lively, bold, and compassionate, so indifferent to fighting and the accumulation of objects and money.

—Brenda Ueland

A musician must make music, an artist must paint, a poet must write if he is ultimately to be at peace with himself. What one can be, one must be.

—Abraham Maslow

A hunch is creativity trying to tell you something.

—Frank Capra

As human beings, our greatness lies not so much in being able to remake the world . . . as in being able to remake ourselves.

—Mahatma Gandhi

So you see, imagination needs moodling—long, inefficient, happy idling, dawdling and puttering.

—Brenda Ueland

When Alexander the Great visited Diogenes and asked whether he could do anything for the famed teacher, Diogenes replied: "Only stand out of my light." Perhaps some day we shall know how to heighten creativity. Until then, one of the best things we can do for creative men and women is to stand out of their light.

—John W. Gardner

The voyage of discovery lies not in finding new landscapes, but in having new eyes.

—Marcel Proust

Given the right circumstances, from no more than dreams, determination, and the liberty to try, ordinary people consistently do extraordinary things. To lead is to create those circumstances.

—Dee Hock

Great improvisers are like priests. They are thinking only of their god.

—Stephane Grapelli

Genius in fact involves sufficient energy and passion to question assumptions that have been taken for granted over long periods.

—David Bohm

You don't see something until you have the right metaphor to let you perceive it.

—Thomas Kuhn

Real artists ship.

—Apple slogan

Straying maps the path.

—Rumi

ARTICLES FOR STUDY CIRCLES ■

Barth, R. S. (2002). The culture builder. *Educational Leadership, 59*(8), 6–11.

DuFour, R. (2004). What is a "professional learning community"? *Educational Leadership, 61*(8), 6–11.

Garmston, R. (1998). Graceful conflict. *Journal of Staff Development, 19*(3).

Kohm, B. (2002). Improving faculty conversations. *Educational Leadership, 59*(8), 31–33.

Noguera, P. A. (2004). Transforming high schools. *Educational Leadership, 61*(8), 26–31.

Sparks, D. (2004). A call to creativity: It's time for us to take the lead in creating change. *Journal of Staff Development, 25*(1), 54–62

Sparks, D. (2004). Broader purpose calls for higher understanding: An interview with Andy Hargreaves. *Journal of Staff Development, 25*(2), 46–50.

Sparks, D. (2004). From hunger to school reform: An interview with Jerry Sternin. *Journal of Staff Development, 25*(1), 46–51.

BOOKS FOR EXTENDED LEARNING ■

Buzan, T. (1974). *Use both sides of your brain.* New York: E. P. Dutton.

Dauten, D. (1996). *The max strategy.* New York: William Morrow.

de Bono, E. (1970). *Lateral thinking.* New York: Harper & Row.

de Bono, E. (1985). *Six thinking hats.* Boston: Little, Brown.

de Bono, E. (1991). *Six action shoes.* New York: HarperCollins.

DePorter, B.. (1992). *Quantum learning: Unleashing the genius in you.* New York: Dell.

Dryden, G., & Vos, J. (1994). *The learning revolution.* Rolling Hills Estates, CA: Jalmar.

Farson, R., & Keyes, R. (2002). *Whoever makes the most mistakes wins.* New York: Free Press.

Garfield, C. (1986). *Peak performers.* New York: Avon.

Gordon, W. J. M. (1961). *Synectics.* New York: Macmillan.

MacKenzie, G. (1996). *Orbiting the giant hairball.* New York: Viking.

Nadler, G., & Hibino, S. (1990). *Breakthrough thinking.* Rocklin, CA: Prima Publishing & Communications.

Pascale, R. (1990). *Managing on the edge.* New York: Simon & Schuster.

Peters, T. (2003). *Re-imagine.* London: Dorling Kindersley.

Stewart, T. A. (1997). *Intellectual capital.* New York: Doubleday-Currency.

Wydro, K. (1981). *Think on your feet.* New York: Prentice Hall.

Zander, B., & Zander, R. S. (2000). *The art of possibility.* Boston: Harvard Business School Press.

Zey, M. (1994). *Seizing the future.* New York: Simon & Schuster.

Film Clips That Explore Keeping Hope Alive

5

If you lose hope, somehow you lose the vitality that keeps life moving, you lose that courage to be, that quality that helps you go on in spite of it all. And so today I still have a dream.

—Martin Luther King, Jr.

John Gardner, the author of *On Leadership* (1990) and a former Secretary of Health, Education, and Welfare, said that one of the main jobs of leaders is to keep hope alive. Without a preferred future in mind it is hard to keep going. We think keeping hope alive is more important today than it ever has been, especially in education. Education is being attacked from many sides while unsung heroes and sheroes are still working in the trenches to help children learn. If a company is under attack, morale and energy wane.

The everyday heroes keep showing up, giving their best, and trying to remain focused on what is important, and that is no easy task when the future is so uncertain in terms of productivity, financial support, and public perception. The leader has to keep attention focused on what is possible, what can be accomplished, and what is working while addressing issues that keep us from reaching the highest potential.

In some schools and businesses a process called *appreciative inquiry* is being used. When we think about how much of our conversations tends to be on what is *not* working and what is *not* right, we can understand how de-energizing the workplace can become. When we focus instead on what is right, there is a more even balance in the whole picture. Speaking about possibilities is more constructive and energy producing. Negative conversations sap energy and reduce creativity.

We think there is a disease in schools called *psychological anorexia*. This debilitating condition can make the most positive people less than effective. In schools where we have worked, staffs get few positive comments from parents, students, and colleagues. We have seen teachers go for five years without a positive comment and still hang in there. Then former students come back to tell them what an impact they made on their lives and how well prepared they were for college. It is amazing to see the body posture and the mental attitude that one comment can make. It is sad that educators go so long without a positive comment and still keep going.

As educators, we do not tell our colleagues about the positives we hear from our students or from other adults. Business is no different. When we do get feedback, it is usually about a problem, not about a positive contribution. We suggest that demonstrating the importance of our colleagues to us and taking the time to say "thank you" to those who help us is extremely important for building relationships and a positive school climate. Tell people specifically how they make your life better or help you do your job better. Balance is important to all of us. A steady diet of negatives will not make us more effective.

So, start the conversation with your own staff, team, or district. None of us got to where we are by ourselves. If mentors worked with you, call them, write them, or e-mail them and express your appreciation. Each of you will benefit from this exchange.

■ CLIPS

Clip: Grant Loses His Way

Themes: Hope, hopelessness, commitment, optimism versus pessimism, the future, determinism, renewal, lost, finding your way, recovering, doubt, efficacy, renewal, quieting negative voices

Film Title & Synopsis: *A Lesson Before Dying* (1999) (TV). This made-for-television movie by HBO is an adaptation of Ernest J. Gaines's novel of the same title. Jefferson (Mekhi Phifer) is wrongly accused of murdering a white storeowner in 1940s Louisiana. In his defense of Jefferson, arguing against the death penalty, his lawyer says, "You might just as soon put a hog in the 'lectric chair as this," stunning Jefferson into depression and appalling his godmother, Miss Emma (Irma P. Hall). Jefferson is subsequently convicted and sentenced to death. Sensing the impact of the lawyer's words on Jefferson and being deeply offended by those words, Miss Emma enlists the help of the community's teacher, Grant Wiggins (Don Cheadle), to convince Jefferson that he is a man, not a hog, so he can die honorably. Grant, Miss Emma, and others visit Jefferson frequently as the story unfolds.

Clip Setup: Grant is having a tough time. Lots of things are getting him down. His conversations with Jefferson at the jail are not going well. Grant is feeling hopeless and discouraged about teaching and the lives of the children, and he's not free to leave because Vivian Baptiste (Lisa Arrindell

Anderson), his girl, is still married. Despite his discouragement, the clip ends with an energized Grant teaching in front of a class and then having a wonderfully hopeful conversation after school with one of his students, Clarence (Elijah Kelley).

Start Movie: 00:32:08 as Grant enters Vivian's classroom with an apple to give her.

Stop Movie: 00:37:04 as Grant's student, Clarence, jumps into the wagon driven by his father and pulls away from the school.

Approximate Length: 5:00

Questions for Discussion:

1. Close to the beginning of the clip, Grant is discouraged and says, "I don't think I wanna teach anywhere anymore!" He then explains why he feels this way. What are some of the factors that have him feeling this way?

2. You have probably felt like that at some point—defeated, hopeless, and powerless. What were the circumstances internally and externally that contributed to your feeling that way? How did you recover?

3. Vivian is the voice of hope and optimism, and she confronts Grant head-on. What is the impact of her sharing her point of view? To what extent are her views "the battle cry of the defeated"?

4. How does the clip end? What is optimistic about it? What is pessimistic about it?

5. Thinking of your work group or school/district, to what extent do you express optimism and hopefulness? How does hope manifest itself in the school/district?

Why We Really Like This Clip: Teaching can be difficult and discouraging. We really like that the portrayal of this teacher's discouragement is genuine. Because the challenge of teaching is only one of the possible stress factors in life, we see in the clip the powerful, complicated, and cumulative interplay of forces that could drag Grant down. Yet, despite it all, we observe Grant at the end of the clip teaching his students and he seems to be a different person, somehow refreshed or rejuvenated, testifying to the satisfaction of teaching. The clip provides an opportunity to examine where that energy comes from and what its nature is. Perhaps educators could talk about how to tap that energy more frequently.

Hope presents itself to teacher Grant Wiggins in the form of Clarence, a smiling student who is fascinated with the globe and who reveals that he does not want to drive the water cart in the fields and says, "One day, Mr. Wiggins, I'm going to go far—far away." It is interesting to us to see how infectious hope is as evidenced in the strength that Grant draws from

Clarence. It is a reminder to us all to focus more frequently on hope, possibility, and optimism, as difficult as it may be. We wonder how we adults can help one another do that more frequently—just as Clarence did it for Grant. The clip presents a chance for teams or schools/districts to talk about focusing more on hope and possibility and designing structures and protocols that can make that happen more frequently.

Notes:

_____

_____

_____

_____

_____

_____

_____

Clip: Speech Against General Smuts' Law

Themes: Constructive channeling of energy, action, hope, self-determination

Film Title & Synopsis: *Gandhi* **(1982).** The film details the life of Mohandas K. Gandhi (Ben Kingsley), a lawyer who transformed himself and the English colony of India. His emphasis on nonviolent resistance becomes the key as he leads the struggle of the Indian people for independence.

Clip Setup: While in South Africa on business, Gandhi commits himself to eliminating a pass system as a means of symbolizing equality. The pass system requires blacks and Indians to carry a government-issued pass at all times—white Europeans are not required to do so. At a rally, he is beaten severely by police with truncheons when he and a group of protestors begin to burn their passes at the public and provocative event. In response, General Smuts, leader and unyielding figurehead of the English colony in Africa, seeks to control any further protests by tightening the pass law to require the fingerprinting of all Indians and to define only Christian marriages as valid. Gandhi speaks to a gathering in a hall, laying out his philosophy and strategy. *Warning:* **This clip contains language that some may find offensive.**

Start Movie: 00:25:41 as a crowd of people sits in a hall, chatting, waiting for Gandhi's speech. Gandhi steps forward to speak.

Stop Movie: 00:31:00 as Gandhi is joined by all the people in the hall in singing "God Save the King."

Approximate Length: 5:17

Questions for Discussion:

1. As Gandhi begins to speak, he welcomes everyone. What is the impact of that? How do you explain the impact?

2. Gandhi also states, to a rousing round of applause, that "we have no secrets." What is the significance of that?

3. A few comments from the audience raise the possibility of violence against the police and other authorities. How is it that Gandhi is able to turn the energy and courage expressed to more productive actions?

4. What is the significance of singing "God Save the King"?

5. How does Gandhi manage to keep hope alive?

6. In schools and other organizations, we sometimes (too often, we're afraid) submit to the less productive way of asserting our different view—saying what we really feel and think in the parking lot after the main meeting or marshaling third- and fourth-party alliances. To what extent are you (as a person, team, school, organization) forthright and honest in your deliberations? What principles do you stand for? And how vigorously do you stand for them?

Why We Really Like This Clip: What we really like about this clip is the way Gandhi is able to change the dynamics of the gathering from hopeless and violent talk to hopeful, principled actions. It is clear after the summary of Smut's law given by Gandhi that the speakers feel that action is required but they are stuck, hopeless. They see violent resistance as their only option. Gandhi, on the other hand, restores hope by praising their courage rather than alienating, chastising, or shaming them. He keeps hope alive by appealing to their bravery, strength, and the rightness of their position as he details a course of action that does not require violence. The immediate action that Gandhi proposes is to take a solemn oath that they will not submit to Smut's law, regardless of the consequences. We think the clip gives teams, departments, and schools/districts a chance to talk about what action is required next—not unlike the Chinese proverb, "Talk doesn't cook rice."

In addition, there is power in symbolism. The oath is a symbol of resistance, of individual and collective strength and direction. It is an affirmation, not a denial, and in that sense the oath is the symbol of creating a new dynamic, not simply the destruction of something old. Teams, schools, and other organizations could use this opportunity to talk about their own symbols—those that exist but shouldn't, those that exist and should, and perhaps those that don't yet exist that need to be created.

We conclude, then, that where conflict is present, it is important to keep hope alive to avoid violence. In your school/districts, in your hearts and souls, where has hope died? Where does it need to be reborn? A hopeful attitude begs lots of questions about working out specific accommodations.

Notes:

_____

_____

_____

_____

_____

_____

_____

Clip: Measuring the Hoop

Themes: Leadership, building on similarities, hope, optimism

Film Title & Synopsis: *Hoosiers* **(1986).** Norman Dale (Gene Hackman) moves to a small Indiana town to teach and to coach the basketball team: the Hickory Huskers. While his past is somewhat obscure and questionable, Dale is clear about his coaching assignment. Challenges and conflicts develop along the way as Dale coaches the team, an underdog, to the state championship. Several critics have called this a "David and Goliath" basketball movie. The film is based on the true story of a 1954 championship team, the Milan (Indiana) Indians.

Clip Setup: The team has made it to the Indiana state finals. As the scene opens, the team is getting off the bus and walking into the huge arena. They are stunned and awed by its size. Sensing this, Coach Dale has a couple of the players measure the height of the hoop and the distance to the foul line. He then reminds them that this is the "same as the gym back in Hickory," where they have been successful.

Start Movie: 1:32:49 as the huge garage door opens, revealing a bus carrying the team into the arena.

Stop Movie: 1:25:36 as Coach Dale says to another adult, half in a whisper, "It's big!" as they depart the arena behind the team to get dressed for practice.

Approximate Length: 2:37

Questions for Discussion:

1. What did you see in the clip? What resonated for you?

2. How did Coach Dale keep hope alive for the team?

3. How important is it to an individual or a group (team, department, school, or organization) to have a sense of hope? What impact does hope have on the individual or group?

4. To what extent are you as an individual, a team, or a school/district hopeful? How is hope shown in specific behaviors?

5. What practices, protocols, procedures, and behaviors promote having hope?

6. What sorts of things eat away at hope? How present are they in your school/district? What is the impact of this dynamic on the people and the school/district?

Why We Really Like This Clip: Students, teachers, and administrators can be awed by their surroundings, especially if they are unfamiliar. This small-town team coming to the big city to play in an arena that seats more than the population of the town itself could have easily psyched out this team. To reduce the anxiety about being in such overwhelming surroundings, Coach Dale brought out a tape measure to make sure his players knew that the court, the height of the hoop, and the length of the foul line were exactly the same as they were at home. There is a bridge here to allow teams, schools, and districts to talk about where they are feeling overwhelmed, frightened, and disoriented and to look for familiar concepts, data, or measurements that will help them get back on track, or center them.

How many times do we let the appearance of the environment cause us to become anxious even though the underlying structures are similar? We think the clip can be used with new teachers to your school or district, to help them to focus on experiences from their history that might have similar dynamics.

This clip also shows how important it is to focus on the field of play. The arena is large, but the basketball court is identical. The clip gives teams an opportunity to talk about what the boundaries are in the field of play. Coach Dale is showing the players that the field of play in the large arena is the same as in the basketball court at home.

Notes:

_____

_____

_____

_____

_____

_____

_____

_____

Clip: Victory in Stories

Themes: Power of story; result of action, hope, legacy, or stewardship; power of the unseen or "soft"; importance of youth

Film Title & Synopsis: *Camelot* **(1967).** Camelot is an adaptation of Lerner and Loewe's stage musical about England's King Arthur (Richard Harris), Guenevere (Vanessa Redgrave), Sir Lancelot Du Lac (Franco Nero), and the famed Round Table. Arthur's goal is to build a civilized, compassionate kingdom where the Round Table serves as a symbol of equality for all the knights who sit there. His goal is frustrated by the machinations of his illegitimate son, Mordred (David Hemmings), jealousies among the knights, and Lancelot and Guenevere's love affair. Yet, a chance encounter with Tom of Warwick (Gary Marsh) transforms his torment over the coming battle to hope.

Clip Setup: King Arthur has just said a final good-bye to Lancelot and seen Guenevere for the last time, because she is going to live in a convent. As Arthur heads back to camp, he is startled by something in the bushes; to his amazement, it is a youngster who is volunteering for military duty— Tom of Warwick. Arthur's conversation with the lad replaces his anguish over his unraveling kingdom with hope for the future.

Start Movie: 2:47:23 as Arthur watches Guenevere leave for the convent and says, "'Bye, dearest love." With that, he turns and starts walking back to his camp.

Stop Movie: 2:54:13 as the sun rises behind the castle for a second or two before the credits start to roll.

Approximate Length: 6:50

Questions for Discussion:

1. What did you observe in the clip? What reactions did you have as you watched the clip?

2. Tom of Warwick is inspired by stories that people tell about the Round Table. What stories inspire you? Your team? Your school/ district?

3. When questioned further by King Arthur, Tom of Warwick says he is inspired by the values of the Round Table. What were they? What values inspire you, your team, or your school/district?

4. In spite of the impending battle, Arthur is hopeful, optimistic. Why?

5. What are the points of optimism in you? Your team? Your school/district?

Why We Really Like This Clip: Arthur says, quite incredulously, "From the stories people tell, you wish to become a knight?" With this question, Arthur begins his journey back to keeping hope alive. For it appeared to Arthur that all was lost—Guenevere was lost to him, the Round Table was in shambles, his most admired friend Lancelot betrayed him and was gone, and the kingdom was at war. But Arthur becomes hopeful about his dream again when he discovers that the dream lives in people's stories and inspires the young. We think the clip gives working groups a chance to talk about their dreams and disappointments and what legacies they wish to leave. The clip also raises the following questions: What stories do we tell to our newest members? How do our stories reflect hope and optimism?

King Pellinore, Arthur's ally, asks of Arthur after the newly knighted Tom of Warwick departs, "Who was that?" Hope restored, Arthur responds enthusiastically to Pelly, "One of what we all are, Pelly. Less than a drop in the great blue motion of the sunlit sea. But it seems that some of the drops sparkle, Pelly. Some of them do sparkle!" How can teams capture the energy that is present in Arthur's enthusiasm and conviction that the future is bright?

Notes:

_____

_____

_____

_____

_____

_____

_____

_____

Clip: Power of Symbolism

Themes: Power of ritual and symbolism, connecting, values, efficacy, optimism, hope

Film Title & Synopsis: *Cider House Rules* **(1999).** The movie is about Homer Wells (Tobey Maguire). He was born and raised just prior to World War II in an orphanage in St. Cloud, Maine, run by the benevolent Dr. Wilbur Larch (Michael Caine). The orphanage is a place where pregnant girls go for an abortion or to give birth and then give up their babies. Homer is essentially raised by Dr. Larch almost like a son and is seen by Larch as his successor. Dr. Larch also imparts his medical knowledge to Homer. But Homer wants a life of his own choosing and leaves the orphanage to seek new experiences. Noteworthy experiences include his relationship with Candy Kendall (Charlize Theron) and the time he spent with an apple-picking crew on a farm owned by Candy's boyfriend, Wally (Paul Rudd).

Clip Setup: Dr. Larch reads to the boys of the orphanage at bedtime. At lights out, he stands at the door, saying, "Good night, you princes of Maine—you kings of New England!"

Start Movie: 00:11:16 as Dr. Larch sits in the middle of the dimly lit room, with single beds lined up against the walls like a military barracks, reading aloud to the boys.

Stop Movie: 00:12:40 as Curley (Spencer Diamond) says, "I like it too," pulling a protective hood down over his head. The scene quickly shifts to a group of girls playing outside in the snow, as one of the girls says, "Watch the door."

Approximate Length: 1:25

Questions for Discussion:

1. As you reflect on the clip, what stands out in your mind?

2. What is it that the boys like about the expression Dr. Larch uses as he leaves the room?

3. How important was the reading ritual to the boys? Generally, how important are rituals? Why are they so important?

4. What rituals do you have in your team or school/district? What do they communicate? How important are they?

5. Are there rituals that should be started? What would they be? What would the new rituals communicate? Why would they be important?

Why We Really Like This Clip: "Good night, you princes of Maine, you kings of New England." During the Depression, when the story takes place, we imagine hope to be a pretty rare commodity. It was probably even scarcer in an orphanage in Maine where couples would only occasionally come to search for a child to adopt. That is why we really like this clip. In 11 words, Dr. Larch manages to convey his hope for their future, referring to them as princes and kings—people of importance and substance. While the world might be rough and uncaring, there was at least one time during the day when someone significant in their life saw for a moment a positive potential and took note of it. We think that the clip offers a unique opportunity to analyze the language used in the workplace: What are the common terms heard? Do they convey hope, possibility, optimism, value—or something else?

We think the ritual is worthy of study to learn how we might duplicate it in an authentic, original way in whatever environment we find ourselves. Ritual seems to be such an important component of a strong community. It connects, recognizes, and celebrates people and their grandest endeavors. We think it would be a great topic for conversation and consideration in teams, schools, and districts. What rituals do we have? Why? How can we create rituals that inspire and appeal to the best in people?

Notes:

_____

_____

_____

_____

_____

_____

_____

Clip: Moon Rising

Themes: Humility, hopeful, thankfulness, optimistic, making a difference

Film Title & Synopsis: *Joe Versus the Volcano* **(1990).** Joe Banks (Tom Hanks) is vaguely depressed by his life. He works in a windowless office with dull walls and fluorescent lighting at a not-very-interesting job and with people who are isolated and quiet. He goes to the doctor often, trying to find the source of his not feeling well. Finally, he is diagnosed by the doctor as having a "brain cloud." It is fatal, but he has a few more months of perfect health before an accelerated debilitation and death. Joe quits his job and is approached shortly thereafter by an eccentric businessman who makes a well-paying proposition that would send Joe to the South Pacific. Joe could "live like a king and die like a man" if he accepts the business-man's proposal. Joe accepts and his journey to the island of Waponi Woo begins. The story involves an assortment of encounters with interesting characters before the completion of the deal: Joe has to jump into a volcano.

Clip Setup: Joe Banks has been diagnosed as having a brain cloud (which is terminal), has quit his job, and has agreed to jump into a volcano in exchange for lots of money to live his last days like a king. On the trip to the South Sea island where the volcano is, the sailboat he is on gets caught in a typhoon that destroys the boat just as Joe jumps into the roiling sea to save his one true love, Patricia Graynamore (Meg Ryan). Joe saves Patricia, though she is unconscious from being struck on the head by a sail boom during the storm. Joe connects some floating suitcases from the sunken boat to make a raft for them. Patricia and Joe are drifting on the open sea on the suitcase platform, hoping to be seen and rescued.

Start Movie: 1:14:27 just as the scene shifts from his shaving to his singing a cowboy song while playing the ukulele.

Stop Movie: 1:18:50 as he falls to the deck after seeing the moon rise.

Approximate Length: 4:26

Questions for Discussion:

1. What did you observe in the clip?

2. What feelings did you have as the clip unfolded?

3. What was Joe saying and feeling?

4. In what ways do you see the experience of Joe with the moon rising as being hopeful?

5. How can you, in your environment, make things more hopeful, more optimistic? What impact(s) would those efforts have?

Why We Really Like This Clip: This is another one of our most favorite clips. Life can be overwhelming with the challenges we have as individuals and organizations. We think the clip offers people working together and individually a chance to climb to a loftier perch and experience a more comforting view of life, appreciating how unique and gifted and big their life is.

We also appreciated the music. It is a strange mix of music. On one hand, it evokes a solitary cowboy image, under the stars on the open range, singing (with a guitar) one of his favorite songs. Oddly, it is open (the ocean instead of the range), solitary (as his girl is unconscious, after being struck by a sail boom as the boat sank), and played not with a guitar but with a ukulele (instrument of the South Seas where he is headed).

We wonder about his delirium as well—when he sees the plastic or neon constellations and rubs his eyes to test and adjust his sight. Are the filmmakers suggesting that we have to be half-delirious from water and food deprivation to see things differently? We think not. We do think it is helpful to do or experience things differently as a prelude to seeing things differently, acting differently. The clip offers teams a chance to talk about doing things differently. In addition, the clip challenges workgroups to plan activities to help team members see things differently.

As this clip involves Joe being stressed by lack of water, food, and amenities, and by exposure to the sun and other elements, it might be easy to overlook the significance of Joe's experience. By saying, "Dear God, whose name I do not know, thank you for my life, I forgot how big. . . . Thank you for my life," Joe seems to be filling his soul with hope that things will work out, that as the moon and sun come up, there is possibility. We see this as an opening for teams to talk about hope no matter how dire the situation looks. This is a truly moving clip.

Notes:

_____

_____

_____

_____

_____

_____

_____

Clip: At Least I Tried

Themes: Persistence, action, commitment, channeling energy

Film Title & Synopsis: *One Flew Over the Cuckoo's Nest* **(1975).** Randle Patrick McMurphy (Jack Nicholson) is a 38-year-old belligerent hell-raiser ("at least five arrests for assault"). He is arrested for statutory rape ("fifteen years old going on thirty-five") and sentenced to prison time. Thinking that time in a mental facility would be easier than time in prison, he fools the authorities into thinking that he needs psychiatric help and is transferred to a mental hospital for evaluation to see if he is indeed mentally ill. While in the hospital, his natural leadership abilities make him a powerful influence on the group of patients. He is an instigator of rebellion among the patients against the rules, procedures, and against his nemesis, Nurse Mildred Ratched (Louise Fletcher).

Clip Setup: A loud argument during a Monopoly game breaks out between Harding (William Redfield) and Taber (Christopher Lloyd) as the other patients look on. McMurphy finally aims a water faucet at the group and sprays the group with water. This causes pandemonium, but most are having fun and the arguing stops. To keep the excitement going,

McMurphy then says that he is going to break out of the place and go downtown for a beer and to watch the World Series. Asked by the group how he is going to do that, McMurphy says he is going to wrestle a giant marble sink stand from the floor, throw it through the window, and walk downtown. He starts taking bets on whether he can do it. *Warning:* **This clip contains language that some may find offensive.**

Start Movie: 00:34:46 as, during a Monopoly game, Taber pokes Harding in the shoulder from behind and baits him to "play the game, Harding."

Stop Movie: 00:39:15 as McMurphy says, "But I tried, didn't I?! At least I did that!" He walks out of the room, angrily kicking a chair out of his way.

Approximate Length: 4:30

Questions for Discussion:

1. What did you see and how did you react while watching the clip?

2. In what sense was McMurphy keeping hope alive?

3. To what extent does attempting seemingly impossible tasks keep hope alive? How would you describe the energy that is created?

4. See if you can articulate situations from your team or school/district that parallel McMurphy's efforts—truly audacious goals or gargantuan tasks. What was the impact on the people and the school/district?

5. What is your opinion about how McMurphy was feeling at the end of the clip? How was the group of patients feeling?

6. What lesson(s) might you take away from this clip?

Why We Really Like This Clip: Randle P. McMurphy is one of our favorite characters. He is risk-taking, irreverent, and irascible. In this clip, he keeps hope alive by organizing a bet around his ability to pick up a sink, crash it through a window, and go downtown for a couple of beers and to watch the World Series. McMurphy gets the other inmates interested in life and the challenge he lays down. While it is his awesome challenge to pry the sink bolted to the floor loose, it is theirs to bet on the outcome and, if he is successful, join him downtown for a few beers. McMurphy gets the other patients interested by dousing them with water as they engage in their argument about petty things. His is an invitation to higher ground, to energy, to challenge, to effort, to the impossible, to his and their bests. While he tried to wrench the sink from its position and ultimately failed, the other inmates watched intently, like there was a possibility that he could actually pull it out. Finally, McMurphy appeals to their own sense of possibility by saying (as he retreats), "But I tried, didn't I?! At least I did that!"

We think the clip could open the discussion in a workgroup about what must be tried but isn't because it looks impossible. The clip also suggests other questions, like: Where are we afraid to try? Or what are some stretch goals we should attempt? What if we fail?

The clip might also suggest a consideration of teamwork as opposed to an individual exerting Herculean efforts while others simply look on, not applying their strength in a common effort. The question for teams might be, How well do we work as a team, or are we individuals exerting our energy and strength in uncoordinated efforts?

Notes:

_____

_____

_____

_____

_____

_____

_____

_____

Clip: Telling the Truth

Themes: Truth telling, persistence, commitment, courage, peer pressure

Film Title & Synopsis: *October Sky* **(1999).** Based on a true story, the film tells the story of Homer Hickam (Jake Gyllenhaal), a high school student from Coalwood, West Virginia. The year is 1957. Homer, like other boys and their fathers before them, is destined to work in the coal mine. On a wonderfully clear night, however, Homer and a group of neighbors observe *Sputnik* crossing the night sky, and Homer is smitten with the idea of flying rockets. At breakfast the morning after the sighting, Homer announces to his family (mom, dad, and brother) that he is going to fly rockets. And so starts the journey of the real Homer Hickam as he and his three friends, Quentin Wilson (Chris Owen), Roy Lee Cook (William Lee Scott), and Sherman O'Dell (Chad Lindberg), with the support of a teacher, Miss Frieda Riley (Laura Dern), learn to build and fly rockets through trial, error, and correction. Beyond the technical side of learning rocketry, pressures from friends, family, and the community toughen and steel their resolve. Although the film ends as Homer and his friends win a National Science Award, Homer goes on to work in NASA's space program.

Clip Setup: The boys had already experimented with rockets close to home, destroying a fence in Homer's yard and almost injuring people as an errant rocket struck Homer's father's office building. Homer's dad was steamed not only about the destruction of mining company property, but because Homer was clearly rejecting mining as an occupation. Homer's father wished his son would follow in his footsteps, as was the custom in Coalwood. So the boys have to move their rocket operation away from town, off the mining company's property. *Warning:* **This clip contains language that some may find offensive.**

Start Movie: 00:21:48 as the scene shifts from Homer picking up his "rocket stuff" in the pouring rain to Quentin holding a book in his hand, in the woods, and Homer saying, "That rocket went up at least 100 feet."

Stop Movie: 00:24:55 as the boys walk down the road, having made amends, toward the place from which they will launch their experimental rockets from then on.

Approximate Length: 3:07

Questions for Discussion:

1. What were your thoughts and reactions as you watched the clip?

2. Homer confronted a real truth—that some of the boys in the group were only half-hearted about their work together. Thinking about his intervention, in your opinion, was it appropriate? Explain. If you were his coach, what would you say to him for feedback?

3. In what sense was Homer keeping hope alive?

4. What was the impact of Homer's intervention?

5. Thinking of your work environment, are there issues that need some truth telling? Explore those situations. What are some strategies and attitudes necessary to make a success of truth telling? What do you anticipate will be the impact on the people and the school/district of truth telling?

Why We Really Like This Clip: Keeping hope alive in the face of overwhelming feedback to quit and take the road already traveled is a difficult task. Even the most committed among us sometimes experience self-doubt. If we are focused on self-doubt at the same time that our support system is negative, that can prove to be too much to handle. How, then, do we find the strength, resolve, and persistence to keep the dream alive? How do researchers continue to look for a cure for cancer, AIDS, and other diseases when progress seems to be slow at best? What are the attributes of staying with your dream in the face of negative feedback? We think these are questions that are very important for adults working in schools and other organizations to address.

The future of our organizations is uncertain. What skills will be required to be successful is also uncertain. What is certain is that we will face increasing challenges in this fast-paced, competitive world economy. We do know that our students will be working in companies in 2010, 2015, and beyond. Having the skills and attitudes to keep hope alive, to persist, and to learn continuously will be enormously useful in an uncertain future. Discussing those attitudes and how to prepare for an uncertain world will be critical for success in the future.

There is another element of this clip that raises extraordinary questions. Think of your work situation. What truth needs to be told? By telling the truth, what opening are you creating for yourself in the future? How can you look reality in the eye and deal with it squarely? Similarly, how can you help others, your teammates or supervisors, see more accurately the truth of a situation? We think this clip gives teams, schools, and districts an invitation to talk about work-related situations with honesty, authenticity, and hope.

Notes:

_____

_____

_____

_____

_____

_____

_____

FIELD WORK: HOW DOES THIS WORK IN REAL TIME WITH REAL PEOPLE? A BEAUTIFUL LIFE

I (WS) was invited to work with a group of principals in a mid-sized urban school district. The invitation came from a consultant who was working with the group. She asked me to deal with the issue of morale. I asked, "How much time do I have?" She said, "About 45 minutes." We both started laughing and agreed it might take two hours to get started on this important issue.

An unpopular new superintendent, a lackluster board of education, consecutive years of huge budget cuts, extensive staff turnover due to a large number of retirements and layoffs, and an unsympathetic legislature promising more cuts were only some of the factors leading to low and sinking morale. When I hear low morale, I immediately think of hopelessness. Sensitive to their challenges, I wanted to make this light but serious, and I wanted them to carry something away that rekindled hope and made their burden a bit lighter.

In my opening remarks, I summarized and explained some of the ideas of two of our favorite trainers: Angeles Arrien (see *The Four-Fold Way: Walking the Paths of the Warrior, Teacher, Healer, and Visionary* [1993]) and Patrick O'Neill (Extraordinary Conversations, Inc., online at http://extraordinary. on.ca/):

- You cannot do this work in the fast lane all the time
- People are arriving exhausted
- STOP the inner terrorism, because it knocks us off the road of meaning
- STOP manufacturing suffering
- Recognize and confront the four demons of insufficiency:
  - I cannot make a difference
  - Other people will never change
  - Circumstances are too powerful
  - There is too much to do

I then told them I was going to show them a short film clip from *Hoosiers*. To set up the experience, I told them that the story was based on a real Indiana basketball team's experience in 1954. I indicated that the team was the underdog all along because they came from a small town, limiting the talent pool of the team. Coach Norman Dale (Gene Hackman) was an outsider and somewhat controversial in the community because he was steadfast about running the team his way, not the way some influential community members wanted. The team finally made it to the state championships.

I explained that the scene takes place as they arrive at the gym for the first time. I invited them to be aware of what was happening on the screen as well as what was happening internally as the scene progressed.

As it was a rather large group of 45 to 50 people, and we were in an old art room with a large screen, I played the tape on two large-screen televisions that the audiovisual department had set up. I cued the tape up the night before, as I knew exactly where I wanted to start the movie.

At the conclusion of the film clip I conducted a large group discussion with questions such as:

- What did you see?
- How did Coach Dale keep hope alive?
- How important is it to have hope?
- What is the impact of having hope on the individual and the group or organization?

Having gotten them involved with the ideas from my opening remarks and the ideas shared after showing the film clip, I passed out an article by

Richard Sagor (2002), "Lessons From Skateboarders," that explains five needs, the fulfilling of which encourages humans to invest in difficult undertakings. I explained the first couple of pages of the article. Then I had the larger group number off by five (1-2-3-4-5 and repeat). I assigned places in the room for the 1's, 2's, and so on, to meet. Each group was asked to read, talk about, and fully understand a section of the article: The 1's would read about competence, the 2's would read about belonging, and so on.

To conclude this part, each group reported their findings to the larger group.

Finally, I concluded my time by asking them to find another person to talk with. They were to think out loud about our experience that day and to plan two or three things they would do today, tomorrow, and by next week that would communicate hope, optimism, confidence, competence, and the like to others they work with.

Here are some of the suggestions for staying balanced and keeping hope alive that came out of the discussion.

- Get a coach similar to the ones business executives have
- Exercise program
- Journal
- Increase humor in the school or district
- Play together; schedule improvisational workshops for staff
- A weekly bulletin named the "Rational Inquirer." The contents are as follows. It starts with a quote accompanied by some reflective questions, usually relating to a thinking or learning theme. The body of announcements is next. Then, add some humor for the staff to read. End the bulletin with a story to touch the soul. Stories, as we have found, help reconnect people with what inspires them. Stories can reignite their passion for teaching and making a difference in students' lives.

IN OTHER WORDS: QUOTES FOR EXTENDING THINKING AND CONVERSATIONS ■

If you want to build a ship, don't herd people together to collect wood and don't assign them tasks and work, but rather teach them to long for the endless immensity of the sea.

—Antoine de Saint-Exupery

Most of the important things in the world have been accomplished by people who have kept on trying when there seemed to be no hope at all.

—Dale Carnegie

I have learned two lessons in my life: first, there are no sufficient literary, psychological, or historical answers to human tragedy, only moral ones.

Second, just as despair can come to one another only from other human beings, hope, too, can be given to one only by other human beings.

—Elie Wiesel

If you lose hope, somehow you lose the vitality that keeps life moving, you lose that courage to be, that quality that helps you go on in spite of it all. And so today I still have a dream.

—Martin Luther King, Jr.

I still believe in Hope—mostly because there's no such place as Fingers Crossed, Arkansas.

—Molly Ivins

The pessimist sees difficulty in every opportunity. The optimist sees the opportunity in every difficulty.

—Winston Churchill

He that lives upon hope will die fasting.

—Benjamin Franklin

Hope is the thing with feathers
That perches in the soul
And sings the tune without the words
And never stops at all.

—Emily Dickinson

The very least you can do in your life is to figure out what you hope for. And the most you can do is live inside that hope. Not admire it from a distance but live right in it, under its roof.

—Barbara Kingsolver

Hope begins in the dark, the stubborn hope that if you just show up and try to do the right thing, the dawn will come. You wait and watch and work: you don't give up.

—Anne Lamott

Hope is not the conviction that something will turn out well, but the certainty that something makes sense regardless of how it turns out.

—Vaclav Havel

A leader is a dealer in hope.

—Napoleon Bonaparte

He who has health has hope; and he who has hope, has everything.

—Arabian Proverb

It is easy to be hopeful in the day when you can see the things you wish on.

—Zora Neale Hurston

Hoping means seeing that the outcome you want is possible and then working for it.

—Bernie S. Siegel

In the midst of winter, I found there was, within me, an invincible summer.

—Albert Camus

Every time you stand up for an ideal, you send forth a tiny ripple of hope.

—Robert Kennedy

The creation of a thousand forests is in one acorn.

—Ralph Waldo Emerson

We'd never know how high we are till we are called to rise; and then, if we are true to plan, our statures touch the sky.

—Emily Dickinson

No pessimist ever discovered the secrets of the stars, or sailed to an uncharted land, or opened a new heaven to the human spirit.

—Helen Keller

ARTICLES FOR STUDY CIRCLES ■

Glickman, C. D. (2003). Symbols and celebrations that sustain education. *Educational Leadership, 60*(6), 34–38.

Goodlad, J. I. (2003). Teaching what we hold sacred. *Educational Leadership, 61*(4), 18–21.

Nieto, S. M. (2003). What keeps teachers going? *Educational Leadership, 60*(8), 14–18.

Sagor, R. (2002). Lessons from skateboarders, *Educational Leadership 60*(1), 34–38.

Sergiovanni, T. J. (2004). Building a community of hope. *Educational Leadership, 61*(8), 33–37.

■ BOOKS FOR EXTENDED LEARNING

Arrien, A. (1993). *The four-fold way: Walking paths of the warrior, teacher, healer, and visionary.* New York: HarperCollins.

Bode, R. (1993). *First you have to row a little boat.* New York: Warner.

Buckingham, M., & Coffman, C. (1999). *First break all the rules.* New York: Simon & Schuster.

Cooper, R. K., & Sawaf, A. (1996*). Executive EQ.* New York: Grosset/Putnam.

Frankl, V. E. (1959). *Man's search for meaning: An introduction to logotheraphy.* New York: Beacon Press.

Gaines, E. J. (1997). *A lesson before dying.* New York: Vintage Books.

Gardner, J. (1990). *On leadership.* New York: Free Press.

Hawley, J. (1993). *Reawakening the spirit in work: The power of Dharmic management.* San Francisco: Berrett-Koehler.

Hendricks, G., & Ludeman, K. (1996). *The corporate mystic.* New York: Bantam Doubleday Dell.

Morrell, M., & Capparell, S. (2001). *Shackleton's way.* New York: Penguin Putnam.

Phillips, D. T. (1992). *Lincoln on leadership: Executive strategies for tough times.* New York: Warner.

Schaef, A. W., & Fassel, D. (1988). *The addictive organization.* San Francisco: Harper & Row.

Seligman, M. E. P. (1990). *Learned optimism.* New York: Knopf.

Siegal, B. S. (1986). *Love, medicine, and miracles.* New York: HarperCollins.

Sparks, D., & Hirsh, S. (1997). *A new vision for staff development.* Alexandria, VA: Association for Supervision and Curriculum Development.

Weisbord, M. R. (1987). *Productive workplaces.* San Francisco: Jossey-Bass.

Film Clips That Explore Change

6

If you don't like change, you're going to like irrelevance even less.

—General Eric Shinseki, Chief of Staff. U.S. Army,
quoted in *Re-Imagine* by Tom Peters (2003)

Change is. Those who do not like change are not going to like the future very much. Most people we know who say they do not want change are usually talking about how fast things are changing and how hard it is to keep up. Depending on our age, we all have a different view of change. Our parents did not have to do much changing. My dad never touched a computer and was very satisfied with a television set. We even remember when our families got our first television sets.

I (Bill, WS) am now 58, and I have stayed in education to retirement. Neither one of us is totally retired. We have learned computers. Skip (WO) is better with technology than Bill. Voice mail, e-mail, and so on were a pain when we first started, but we have adapted. Our children are on a very short change cycle. Three to five years is about the average length of employment or interest in anything these days. Our children are looking at 10 to 12 different jobs in five to seven different organizations and two to three different careers. Their children will be on an even shorter change cycle.

We bemoan the fact that we have to change, but the fact is that we are changing all the time, always adapting to new products, ideas, and situations. The world continues to change faster than we can handle. New threats to peace, health, and prosperity are constant.

We are tired of hearing that educators will not change. The fact is, educators have been changing all the time, due to changing family structures, changing demographics, ever-increasing poverty, continuing reductions in budgets, new demands from society and legislatures, and the list goes on. Educators adapt and change yearly, monthly, daily, and sometimes even hourly. Rarely is one day like another. We think educators are very adaptable, but the demands are outpacing time, money, and energy. In addition, Peter Senge is right when he says that people do not resist change, they resist being changed.

So, the question isn't whether we are going to change; the question is, How will we deal with change? If we refine that question a little further, we could ask, Do we have the skills to constantly adapt to a changing world? As leaders, how do we get ready for, proactively plan for, and lead change?

There are many resources on change that we will mention. The film clips that we have organized for you can help you to discuss change and thereby set up more opportunities for you to lead change in your own situation.

■ CLIPS

Clip: I'm Getting Married

Themes: Conflict, self-control, mental models, feedback

Film Title & Synopsis: *Father of the Bride* **(1991).** George (Steve Martin) is a man who loves his town, house, job, family, and life just as they are. He does not want change. However, his 21-year-old daughter, Kimberly (Annie Banks), comes home from a semester of study in Europe to announce that she is going to marry Bryan MacKenzie (George Newburn). George is not pleased with the prospect of losing his daughter to a man he knows nothing about. Nor is he pleased with the costs associated with the wedding. In the planning of the wedding, his wife Nina (Diane Keaton) and son Matty (Kieran Culkin) help George deal with conflict and change.

Clip Setup: The whole family is under one roof again. George is feeling quite good and is lining up social events (concerts, games) that the family can do together. No longer able to contain her excitement, Kimberly announces that she is getting married, and George loses it while Matty and Nina look on.

Start Movie: 00:08:34 as the family sits at the table and George is trying to arrange a schedule of family activities.

Stop Movie: 00:14:00 as George leaves the table to go after his daughter.

Approximate Length: 5:32

Questions for Discussion:

1. What behaviors made George's life worse?

2. What might he have done differently?

3. What signs could George have recognized as tips that he needed to pay closer attention?

4. Consider change in your work environment. What behaviors make your life worse? What might you do differently?

5. Thinking of your work environment, what behaviors would help you deal with change constructively? What behaviors would inhibit constructive engagement with change?

Why We Really Like This Clip: Change can be difficult, and the more comfortable you are, the less you like change. The devil known is better than the devil unknown. The problem is that you cannot control others. The only person you can control is yourself. George wants everything to return to normal but finds that his little girl is going to get married. Of course, rarely are things the way they used to be. The way George deals with change is similar to the way adults deal with change in the workplace. Some things probably should not change. However, many changes are happening all the time. Many, like Kimberly's growing up and getting married, are beyond our control. The only leverage we can exert is how we respond to what is changing. Our response helps or hinders.

We think this clip can start the conversation with staff about what changes are occurring, reactions to those changes, and what strategies and actions will be necessary to respond proactively and positively to the changes. The personal connection can be used as a bridge to look at organizational changes.

Notes:

_____

_____

_____

_____

_____

_____

_____

Clip: Between Your Knees

Themes: The bureaucracy, rules, alienation, protest, creativity, the power to get what you want

Film Title & Synopsis: *Five Easy Pieces* **(1970).** Robert Dupea (Jack Nicholson) is an interesting but distant person whose character is revealed throughout the film. While he is an oil rigger living with his waitress girlfriend Rayette (Karen Black), he spends his time drinking beer, chasing women, and generally living an irresponsible life. Dupea finds out from his sister that their father, who lives in Washington state, has had a stroke and is not expected to live long. He leaves for the Washington coast, taking

Rayette with him on this extended road trip that is filled with interesting vignettes and characters. Haunted by a failed childhood (he was not the gifted piano player his father wanted) and on the run from himself, his past, and his family, he winds up trying to talk to his father before he dies. The end of the movie sees Robert Dupea running away from Rayette and all his other difficulties.

Clip Setup: Dupea and his girlfriend, Rayette, are on their way to Washington state to see Dupea's ailing father, perhaps for the last time. Along the way, they happen onto a car that has run off the road. They agree to give Palm Apodaca (Helena Kallianiotes) and Terry Grouse (Toni Basil), occupants of the wrecked car, a lift. After an argument about nothing at all in the car between Rayette and Palm Apodaca, Dupea heads for a café for a break.

Start Movie: 00:45:03 as Dupea and Rayette are sitting in a booth in a restaurant with a waitress poised to take their order.

Stop Movie: 00:46:58 as Palm Apodaca says, "I would have just punched her out," and the scene shifts to cars on the highway as music plays.

Approximate Length: 1:56

Questions for Discussion:

1. What thoughts and feelings did you experience as you watched the scene?

2. The confrontation did not yield the result that Dupea wanted: his toast. Why? Given the circumstances, were there other ways to have dealt with the situation? What ways might have yielded the results he wanted?

3. Thinking of your own work environment, identify a time when you did not get the results you required. Think of the interaction between the parties. What other possibilities are there that might have made you successful?

4. Think of a meeting or a project you have coming up where you have a desired outcome. What are some strategies you could employ to increase the likelihood of your success?

Why We Really Like This Clip: Change is tricky business. Change requires that people think differently and do different things. Rules may need to be broken. Egos get involved. Turf is protected and transgressed. Yet change agents must control themselves, even if they cannot control the situation and other people. We really like this clip because it calls attention to achieving our goals through self-management, especially when dealing with others and "the establishment." It is clear that Dupea had "fun" at the waitress's expense, but he failed to get what he wanted—the toast. While he was trying on one hand to make it easy for her to "break the rules," he did it in such a way as to alienate her, foreclosing on his chance of success.

He might have been successful had he not told her to "hold it between her knees." In other words, he failed to manage himself and the situation successfully in order to get what he wanted. In addition, none of them got to eat, as Dupea cleared the table with his arm, sending glasses and dishes crashing to the floor as they left the café.

This clip offers teams and organizations an opportunity to see the importance of relationships in realizing aspirations. The film clip could help team members see that everyone plays a role in the achievement or failure and that, whether we like it or not, we are interdependent.

Notes:

_____

_____

_____

_____

_____

_____

_____

Clip: The Boys in the Barber Shop

Themes: Conflict, self-knowledge, confidence, handling one's self

Film Title & Synopsis: *Hoosiers* (1986). Norman Dale (Gene Hackman) moves to a small Indiana town to teach and to coach the basketball team. While his past is somewhat obscure and questionable, Dale is clear about his coaching assignment. Challenges and conflicts develop along the way as Dale coaches the underdog team to the state championships. This film is based on the true story of a 1954 championship team.

Clip Setup: "This town doesn't like change much. So we thought we'd get together here tonight and show ya how we do things here." There you have the purpose of the meeting right from a character's mouth in the clip. You see the men of the town and Coach Dale begin to explore their new relationship at the barber shop.

Start Movie: 00:08:33 as a citizen asks, "Last time you coached was twelve years ago?"

Stop Movie: 00:10:17 as Coach Dale thanks the assembled group and exits the barbershop.

Approximate Length: 1:44

Questions for Discussion:

1. What would you say about the way Coach Dale handled himself? How effective was his interaction?

2. What specific behaviors do you observe that control the situation, making destructive conflict avoidable? To what extent are those behaviors practiced in your department, team, or organization?

3. What messages seem to be aimed at Coach Dale from the men in the barbershop? What are some of the veiled messages aimed at you in your work environment? How do you normally handle the messages—how do you normally handle yourself?

4. What seemed to be some of the assumptions that people were making?

5. What do you suppose the conversation was after Coach Dale excused himself?

6. To what extent were these things present in the scene: respect, civility, thoughtfulness, warmth, welcome? To what extent are they present in your work environment?

7. How could things have gone differently?

Why We Really Like This Clip: This clip is a perfect example of how cultural norms are passed on through generations and groups acculturate new people. Think of how new teachers are integrated into your school, system, or organization. Do you see new people as a resource to help you expand your own repertoire, or do you see new people as those who have to learn your way of doing things? Will they be accepted if they have a different way of doing things, or will they be shunned and shamed until they come around to your way? How you treat new staff members and how you honor them when they enter the system tells many things about your culture. Is this an opportunity or a threat? The clip offers a great opening to talk about how we treat or initiate others into our work settings—teams, departments, schools, or organizations.

We think this clip can be used for new teacher/employee orientation, for teaching new mentors for new teachers, and as a discussion topic for designing high-quality professional development for new staff members. What is an example of your own barbershop?

Notes:

_____

_____

_____

_____

_____

_____

_____

_____

Clip: Surrender

Themes: Reflection; coaching; listening; logic versus deeper, intuitive principles; hope; surrender; grace

Film Title & Synopsis: *Cast Away* **(2000).** Chuck Noland (Tom Hanks) is a systems engineer troubleshooter for FedEx. He flies all over the world fixing the broken planes in the FedEx system that moves packages. His life is run so much by the clock that his fiancée, Kelly Frears (Helen Hunt), gives him her grandfather's railroad watch as he hops another plane. Noland hitches a ride on a FedEx plane to his latest project in Moscow. The plane crashes after an explosion onboard. He is the only survivor and spends the next four years stranded on an island in the South Pacific. Noland finally gets the chance to escape when a piece of debris washes ashore that can be used as a crude sail. He returns home to reacquaint himself with his friends and go back to working for FedEx and learns that his fiancée has married someone else and now has a family.

Clip Setup: Finally home after his solitary four-year ordeal on the island, Noland finds that his fiancée, Kelly, is married and has a family. On a rainy night, Noland goes to Kelly's house to see her for the first time since his return. It is clear by the end of the meeting that it is finished between them, and, sadly, it is time for both of them to move on. He feels the weight of this and goes to a friend's house just to talk. We observe him talking to his friend.

Start Movie: 2:08:11 as the scene changes from a car pulling up the driveway on a rainy night to a hand holding a liquor glass as Noland says, "We both had done the math."

Stop Movie: 2:12:06 right after Noland says, "Who knows what the tide could bring?" and lingers on those words before the scene shifts abruptly to Noland driving along the open road listening to Elvis Presley on the radio.

Approximate Length: 3:55

Questions for Discussion:

1. What were your reactions and thoughts as you watched the clip?

2. What did Noland describe?

3. Noland describes a change that came over him. He essentially quit fighting his circumstances and instead surrendered to them, without giving up on life, hope, or possibility. Thinking about your work environment, are there times when it is appropriate to surrender? Express your thinking.

4. Although he's sad that he lost his love, Noland is clear about what he has to do: keep breathing. He seems to be saying that where there is a breath, there is possibility and hope. To what extent is that applicable to your work life?

Why We Really Like This Clip: This is one of our favorite clips because it stresses the value of surrender in dealing with changing situations. Clearly Noland was in the middle of a life-changing dilemma, being stuck on the island with only the slimmest of chances for rescue. He had lost all hope. He could control nothing but the time and place of his own death—and he found that he didn't even have power over that. It reminds us of how important power and control are in a changing situation and how counterproductive it is to deny and struggle against that which you cannot control. Humans revert to power and control as a way of dealing with change, and the more fundamental, awkward, and profound the change is, the more we want to control it. We think that that approach makes us less supple, creative, and able to deal effectively with change.

We should take a lesson from Noland. The strange calm he reports that came over him (he describes it as a warm blanket) after his surrender to the situation actually freed him to hope again and to be aware of openings to escape as they showed themselves. Surrendering made the situation livable, better—and he could still hold on to the hope of getting off the island and even plan his escape. His focus became living as well as he could—he had to keep breathing. The lesson for us is that there is great power in surrender. By surrendering we are able to recognize and accept the situation and free ourselves to be more flexible, graceful, and intelligent. It enables us to engage the situation on a different level—without being angry, hostile, resentful, cynical, or pessimistic. Surrender is also qualitatively different from giving up, which is a withdrawal from the situation and from life into an egocentric corner. Now that he faces another life-altering challenge—a life without Kelly—Noland has learned that he has to keep breathing and look for the sunrise tomorrow. And, "Who knows what the tide will bring?"

Notes:

_____

_____

_____

_____

_____

_____

_____

_____

Clip: I Quit

Themes: Change, observing, listening to one's self, bargains made, acting on beliefs, value of one's life

Film Title & Synopsis: *Joe Versus the Volcano* (1990). Joe Banks (Tom Hanks) is vaguely depressed by his life. He works in a windowless office with dull walls and fluorescent lighting at a not-very-interesting job and with people who are isolated and quiet. He goes to the doctor often, trying to find the source of his not feeling well. Finally, he is diagnosed by Dr. Ellison (Robert Stack) as having a "brain cloud." It is fatal, but he has a few more months of perfect health before an accelerated debilitation and death. Joe quits his job and is approached shortly thereafter by an eccentric businessman who makes a proposition that would send Joe to the South Pacific. Joe could "live like a king and die like a man" if he accepts the businessman's proposal. Joe accepts and his journey to the island of Waponi Woo begins. The story involves an assortment of encounters with interesting characters before the completion of the deal: Joe has to jump into a volcano.

Clip Setup: Joe Banks has just been told that he is terminally ill with a "brain cloud." The doctor advises him that he has some time left and should live it well. The world looks very different to him now—he has been shocked out of vague malaise and complacency and is infused with a new energy of mindfulness. After all, he is convinced that he does not have much time left, and it is apparent when he gets back to the office. After doing odd things in the outer office (like having an arm-wrestling match with a mannequin's arm and messing up Mr. Waturi's [his boss's] hair with the same arm), Joe walks into his own office, followed by Waturi. *Warning:* **This clip contains language that some may find offensive.**

Start Movie: 00:19:52 as Mr. Frank Waturi (Dan Hedaya), Joe's boss, comes through a door, pointing with the hand of a mannequin, and says, "Joe, don't touch that! What are you doing?"

Stop Movie: 00:23:34 as Dede (Meg Ryan), the office secretary, says with a smile on her face, "Wow, what a change!"

Approximate Length: 3:42

Questions for Discussion:

1. What did you find most interesting in this clip?

2. In your opinion, is it only by crisis that people wake up to different perceptions or possibilities? Explain.

3. What are some of the things that Mr. Waturi says that communicate to Joe that he is nothing special?

4. Joe made a bargain with "the job" because he was too afraid to live his own life; so he sold it to Waturi for "three hundred freakin' dollars a week." What are some of the bargains you make at work? What is the impact on the school/district and individuals of the bargains you have made?

5. Obviously, bargains are necessary. What are elements of a healthy work bargain? How should one deal with the bargain that has gone sour?

6. How can people live healthier work lives?

Why We Really Like This Clip: We do so like the energy in this clip. Here is a man who has been stunned to life by a terminal diagnosis. Things that used to be important (prohibitive signs on drain pipes, references, a job) suddenly have been replaced by books, a ukulele, a desk lamp he loved, and the realization that he has wasted his limited time and wishes he had some of that time back now. Joe observes that he has sold his life for $300 a week because he was fearful of taking a chance. We are reminded of a line in one of Bob Dylan's songs that observes that, if a person is not continually growing and recreating, he is actually dying. And here is a man who is in the throes of being reborn. The clip gives people a chance to talk about what has heart and meaning, what is important, and how to rekindle those frequently dormant energies.

For us, the clip is noteworthy because it challenges us to be more authentic and more present. We need to question more frequently and thoroughly the "agreements" we make in the name of stability, not "ruffling feathers," and safety. The clip offers the opportunity to examine those agreements to see if they are value-based or fear-based. Joe was clearly moving from fear to value in this clip, and the energy-creating potential is enormous, as we can see. How can we get more of this scarce commodity into our workplaces?

Joe also becomes more sensitive to his environment, having ignored it for some time. He comments on the taste of the coffee, the presence of an attractive woman, the florescent lights, and the health of his boss and coworkers. How many days do we go through life ignoring the little things? As doctor and author Jon Kabat Zinn says, "The little things? The little moments? They aren't little."

Notes:

_____

_____

_____

_____

_____

_____

_____

Clip: Chocolates Assembly Line

Themes: Dealing with change, feedback, supervision, leadership, teamwork

Film Title & Synopsis: *Best of I Love Lucy, Volume 2* **(1951).** This is the classic Episode 39 where Lucy, Ethel, Ricky, and Fred decide to switch roles: The girls will go out and get jobs while the men stay home and manage their households. Though ill prepared and inexperienced for most of what the employment office has to offer in the world of work, the girls finally manage to get jobs at Kramer's Candy Kitchen while Fred and Ricky manage the household duties. Disaster occurs in both places, so they decide to call the whole thing off and go back to a "normal" life, the way things used to be.

Clip Setup: Unsuccessful at a number of the jobs they were assigned in the candy factory, Lucy and Ethel finally wind up on an assembly line, wrapping individual candy pieces. This is their last chance—if one piece of candy gets by them, they will be fired.

Start Movie: 00:17:13 as the supervisor walks in the door with Lucy and Ethel behind her and shows them the conveyor belt that the chocolates will be on.

Stop Movie: 00: 20:17 as Lucy fills her shirt with candies.

Approximate Length: 3:04

Questions for Discussion:

1. What observations would you make about the clip?

2. What were the elements of the situation that made failure likely? Having identified the failure-producing elements, explore the possibility that there are some of those same elements in your own workplace. What are they?

3. How did Lucy and Ethel deal with change? What similarities do you see in your own workplace dealing with change?

4. What might Lucy and Ethel have done to make the situation more successful? How can you be more successful in dealing with change in your school/district?

5. As you think about change in your team or school or organization and the film clip, what should you keep in mind as you go about your business?

6. What factors promote successful change? What factors inhibit successful change? Which of those factors are operating in your environment today? How can you increase your chances of success?

Why We Really Like This Clip: We liked the portrayal of the "organization" when the supervisor says, "Let 'er roll!" and the conveyor belt does not move. This is a concrete example of parts of the organization not talking to, planning with, or communicating with other parts of the organization. We have found in our work that people frequently do not spend nearly enough time talking and planning with one another, and the result is less effectiveness.

It is interesting to note that the supervisor concluded that "somebody's asleep at the switch" rather than the switch is broken or there is a problem in the other department. The clip provides an opportunity for teams, departments, schools, and other organizations to talk about "personalizing" problems or blaming people rather than looking for a solution to the "system's" trouble.

Another feature of the clip we really like is the false sense Ethel and Lucy have that "this is easy" and "we can handle this OK." Of course the judgments were based on the idea that things were going to stay as they were. Soon, however, it became clear that change was afoot and the belt was moving faster. They were falling behind. To their credit, Lucy and Ethel did try new behaviors to keep up—eating some candy, dropping some, and eventually stuffing their clothing with candy, all to no avail, for as the belt moved along and they got farther behind, the quality of their work diminished and they could not keep up. What was needed was not the same behavior faster, but a different strategy—maybe communication with the person or team in the other room controlling the belt speed or a conversation with the supervisor. The clip offers a chance to talk about the assumptions we make about our comfortable, current reality; what possible changes we could make; and how we can best accommodate change.

Still another feature we found interesting was the reaction of Lucy and Ethel to the supervisor. Granted, this was a high-stakes situation in that they would be fired if they failed. Instead of telling the truth to the supervisor (who was not present on the line), they hid their mistakes and performance problems, leading the supervisor to conclude erroneously that they were working splendidly—so the line could be sped up a little with no difficulty. The supervisor looked at the process instead of the result and drew a flawed conclusion. The clip offers a chance for teams and school/districts to talk about how they handle failure, data about operations or results, and mistakes.

Notes:

_____

_____

_____

_____

_____

_____

_____

FIELD WORK: HOW DOES THIS WORK IN REAL TIME WITH REAL PEOPLE? A FUNNY THING HAPPENED ON THE WAY TO THE FORUM

Change in schools is happening at a faster pace than most are comfortable with. Changes in curriculum, in rules and regulations, and in personnel make us even more susceptible to FUDs (fears, uncertainties, and doubts). The unfortunate thing is that schools are never going to be the same as they were in every respect. We all hope they stay the hope of students and parents to prepare children for their future. However, outside demands will require changes in structure, in results, and techniques for teaching wider learning styles and diversity.

In one district where I (WS) worked, the district started a site-based management initiative. There was a good deal of misapprehension because the district office did not give concrete mandates about the structure of the councils or the processes to be used in creating the councils. We were given general guidelines that included the size of the council (8–12 members), the need to be gender and culturally mixed, the need to include community members as well as parents, and the need to meet on a monthly basis.

We struggled to get a council together, and the anxiety was then transferred to the elected council. Who were all these new members? What was our purpose? How would we operate? What happens if we fail? Why are we doing this? All of these unanswered questions were gnawing at these strangers.

As principal of the school and the initial convener of the group, I decided to include the clip from *Father of the Bride*, "I'm Getting Married," in our first session. After all, it is a humorous look at someone who loved things the way they were and really did not want any part of the change that was thrust on him. The clip might lighten things up and create a space for us to start talking about change.

We had scheduled a two-hour time slot for our initial meeting. Because the meeting was at night (7–9 p.m.) to accommodate working parents and community members who had day jobs, I made sure there were treats to say thanks for putting in the extra time and that we're in this together—let's get some enjoyment out of this stressful situation.

I prepared a sheet of a dozen or so quotes and had copies for everyone at the tables. The sheets with the quotes were at their places when the participants sat down before the meeting started. I thought they might look them over.

I started the meeting by welcoming everyone and tried to give some optimistic, encouraging words. I asked all participants to briefly introduce themselves to the group (name, connection to the school, interests) and to tell which quote had meaning for them and why. I wanted everyone's voice in the room, I wanted to start talking about something important yet not threatening, and I wanted to seed the conversation with the concept of change, because that is what we would be dealing with during the next couple of hours.

After that, I explained that change was not always planned, that sometimes it is thrust on us, much like in our situation. I told them it reminded me of a favorite scene of mine from a motion picture and that I would like to show it to them. I told them the story, who the characters were, and what was happening as we entered the scene. I thought it was important for them to have as much information about the clip to make it eminently understandable. I asked them to be aware of not only what was happening on the screen, but also to track what was happening inside themselves as well.

As we were a small group, I had a VCR/TV combination in the room. I had cued up the tape the night before to the place where I wanted to begin.

After viewing the clip, we talked about our impressions and other questions. Some offered stories of similar things happening to them. Then I asked about their apprehensions, misgivings, and fears about being involved in our little adventure. I listed these on chart paper. I then asked if there were any similarities between our list and what George (Steve Martin) was feeling—there were real similarities. We continued by focusing on what attitudes or behaviors George could have engaged in that would have made the situation healthier. Finally I asked what attitudes and behaviors would make our situation healthier. All this was listed on chart paper as well, and the list became part of our work together.

We decided that attitudes and behaviors could become "norms" for our group and that we would post them at our meetings as a reminder to ourselves.

Finally, as 9 p.m. approached, I handed out an article, "Why Change Is So Challenging for Schools: An Interview With Peter Senge" (Sparks, 2001) that appeared in the *Journal of Staff Development* and asked that they read this before the next meeting as a way to begin thinking about the changes we would be involved in at the school. I concluded by asking for a volunteer who would facilitate the discussion of the article at the next meeting.

IN OTHER WORDS: QUOTES FOR EXTENDING THINKING AND CONVERSATIONS ■

The art of progress is to preserve order amid change and to preserve change amid order.

—Alfred North Whitehead

It doesn't work to leap a twenty-foot chasm in two ten-foot jumps.

—American proverb

How wonderful it is that nobody need wait a single moment before starting to improve the world.

—Anne Frank

In times of change, learners inherit the Earth, while the learned find themselves beautifully equipped to deal with a world that no longer exists.

—Eric Hoffer

Everyone thinks of changing the world, but no one thinks of changing himself.

—Leo Tolstoy

The truth is that our finest moments are most likely to occur when we are feeling deeply uncomfortable, unhappy, or unfulfilled. For it is only in such moments, propelled by our discomfort, that we are likely to step out of our ruts and start searching for different ways or truer answers.

—M. Scott Peck

Never doubt that a small group of thoughtful, committed citizens can change the world. Indeed, it is the only thing that ever has.

—Margaret Mead

It's not so much that we're afraid of change or so in love with the old ways, but it's that place in between that we fear. . . . It's like being between trapezes. It's Linus when his blanket is in the dryer. There's nothing to hold on to.

—Marilyn Ferguson

Know what's weird? Day by day, nothing seems to change, but pretty soon . . . everything's different.

—Calvin from "Calvin and Hobbes"

Be the change you want to see in the world.

—Mahatma Gandhi

Things do not change; we change.

—Henry David Thoreau

It is not necessary to change. Survival is not mandatory.

—W. Edwards Deming

It is not the strongest of the species that survive, nor the most intelligent, but the one most responsive to change.

—Charles Darwin

Any real change implies the breakup of the world as one has always known it, the loss of all that gave one an identity, the end of safety.

—James Baldwin

Life is change. Growth is optional. Choose wisely.

—Anonymous

Just because we cannot see clearly the end of the road, that is no reason for not setting out on the essential journey. On the contrary, great change dominates the world, and unless we move with change we will become its victims.

—John F. Kennedy

Resistance to change does not reflect opposition, nor is it merely a result of inertia. Instead, even as they hold a sincere commitment to change, many people are unwittingly applying productive energy toward a hidden competing commitment. The resulting dynamic equilibrium stalls the effort in what looks like resistance but is in fact a kind of personal immunity to change.

—Robert Kegan and Lisa Laskow Lahey

One doesn't discover new lands without consenting to lose sight of the shore for a very long time.

—Andre Gide

Faced with the choice between changing one's mind and proving that there is no need to do so, almost everybody gets busy on the proof.

—John Kenneth Galbraith

There is a time for departure even when there's no certain place to go.

—Tennessee Williams

One isn't necessarily born with courage, but one is born with potential. Without courage, we cannot practice any other virtue with consistency. We can't be kind, true, merciful, generous, or honest.

—Maya Angelou

No one can persuade another to change. Each of us guards a gate of change that can only be opened from the inside. We cannot open the gate of another, either by argument or by emotional appeal.

—Marilyn Ferguson

ARTICLES FOR STUDY CIRCLES ■

Brandt, R. (2003). Is your school a learning organization? 10 ways to tell. *Journal of Staff Development, 24*(1), 10–16.

Bryk, A. S., & Schneider, B. (2003). Trust in schools: A core resource for school reform. *Educational Leadership, 60*(6), 40–44.

Copland, M. A., & Boatright, E. E. (2004). Leading small: Eight lessons for leaders in transforming large comprehensive high schools. *Phi Delta Kappan, 85*(10), 762–770.

Feiman-Nemser, S. (2003). What new teachers need to learn. *Educational Leadership, 60*(8), 25–29.

Fullan, M. (2002). The change leader. *Educational Leadership, 59*(8), 16–20.

Richardson, J. (2001, August-September). Learning teams: When teachers work together, knowledge and rapport grow. *Tools for Schools,* pp. 1–2.

Shulla-Cose, D., & Day, K. (2003). Shaping a school culture. *Educational Leadership, 61*(4), 88–89.

Sparks, D. (2001). Change: It's a matter of life or slow death. An interview with Robert Quinn. *Journal of Staff Development, 22*(4), 49–53.

Sparks, D. (2001). Why change is so challenging for schools: An interview with Peter Senge. *Journal of Staff Development, 22*(3), 42–47.

Sparks, D. (2003). The answer to "when?" is "now." An interview with Peter Block. *Journal of Staff Development, 24*(2), 52–55.

■ BOOKS FOR EXTENDED LEARNING

Ackoff, R. L. (1991). *Ackoff's fables.* New York: John Wiley.

Ackoff, R. (1999). *Re-creating the corporation.* New York: Oxford University Press.

Argyris, C. (1990). *Overcoming organizational defenses.* New York: Prentice Hall.

Fritz, R. (1984). *The path of least resistance.* New York: Ballantine.

Fullan, M. (1993). *Change forces.* London: Falmer Press.

Fullan, M. (2001). *Leading in a culture of change.* San Francisco: Jossey-Bass.

Hall, G. E., & Hord, S. M. (2001). *Implementing change: Patterns, principles, and potholes.* Needham Heights, MA:Pearson.

Hamel, G. (2000). *Leading the revolution.* Boston: Harvard Business School Press.

Johnson, S. (1998). *Who moved my cheese?* New York: Penguin Putnam.

Land, G., & Jarman, B. (1992). *Break-point and beyond.* New York: Harcourt Brace Jovanovich.

O'Reilly, K. W. (Ed). (1995). *Managing the rapids—Stories from the forefont of the learning organization.* Cambridge, MA: Pegasus.

O'Toole, J. (1995). *Leading change.* San Francisco: Jossey-Bass.

Pascale, R. T., Millemann, M., & Gioja, L. (2000). *Surfing the edge of chaos.* New York: Crown Business.

Peters, T. K. (2003). *Re-imagine! Business excellence in a disruptive age.* London: Dorling Kindersley.

Pritchett, P. (1994). *New work habits for a radically changing world.* Dallas: Pritchett.

Afterword

As we developed this book, the mood of the country continued to be polarized. For the sake of the students, for the sake of the staff who work with those students, and for the sake of our country, we hope these film clips lead to helpful conversations among adults, create positive plans of action, and cause learning by reflection for educational professionals.

There is a solid belief by a majority of the American public in the value and importance of public education. While the very concept of public education seems to be under attack by advocates of charter schools, the privatization movement, the testing mania motivated by political agendas, and accountability through newspaper articles, and while there are misgivings about some features of public education, there is a solid core of support for the idea of public education. Despite the challenges, there is a strong cadre of professionals and public advocates who have a fundamental belief in the purpose and necessity of public education. A host of prominent, intelligent people see public schools as indispensable to our democratic way of life. Schools are the common experience—the crossroad—for most of our children, where people of different backgrounds meet and are strangers no more.

Hidden in the swirling confusion of the challenges, however, are some powerful, positive currents. For example, there is profound work being done on brain-based learning. There is an increasing body of knowledge about best practice and professional learning communities and creating positive learning cultures in schools. And, as in the computer and technological revolution of the 1980s and 1990s, progress and payoff are not immediately or readily apparent. It takes time to develop appropriate protocols, practices, and insights to take advantage of the new ideas. What very well could be born out of this angst and chaos is a much stronger, effective system of public education. We did not say it would be easy, just worth it.

Resource

Some Pretty Firm Guidelines for Using Film Clips in Training

1. **View the clip before using it.** Teachers and trainers know that the last thing they want is an unforeseen surprise to ruin the training experience.

2. **Introduce the movie that the clip is taken from.** Make sure you tell the participants the name, a bit about the characters, the plot, and the context. Remember—you want to have the participants focus on what you want, rather than have them struggling to tie things together that you could have given them ahead of time.

3. **Set up the clip.** It is easy to forget to do this in the anticipation of an exciting experience, especially when you are focusing on pushing the right button on the videotape machine. This may take some finesse. On the one hand, you want to orient the participants so they see and understand what is going on, who is interacting, where they are, and so on. But you do not want to give them so much that you take away the mystery, anticipation, or fascination.

4. **Give them instructions on what to look for.** In most cases, the instruction will involve noticing something in the film, that is, how a problem is handled, how tension is resolved, or what you are trying to point out—related to why you chose to show the clip. Frequently, however, it is helpful to tell participants to be aware of what is going on in themselves as well, as they tend to get caught up in the clip and ignore what is happening inside them.

5. **Warn participants if the clip contains language that some may find offensive.** Err on the side of caution; if there is any question, tell them ahead of time. They will appreciate your sensitivity to the issue. Because this book focuses on training adults, difficulties will probably be minimal, if there are any at all.

6. **Cue the clip up ahead of time.** A good time to do this is the night before your session. Take the time to find the spot in the movie where you want to begin. Have a firm idea of where you want to

stop the clip. Some of the clips lend themselves to being started before the notation in this book, and some lend themselves to being stopped beyond the notation in the book. It is important that you be clear about what you want.

7. **Review the clip before using it.** What we mean is, take the time to review the clip even if you have used it a number of times before. You may have forgotten some of its features, or you may see something new.

8. **Practice being flexible.** You will find that adults often have unique ways of interpreting what they see. If you are flexible, you will be able to extend the discussions you have and your insights into the clip. It could be helpful in your interactions with and among participants.

9. **Debrief—let the participants talk about what they saw and how it applies to them and their work.** Reflection is paramount for adults, so letting them respond to questions, explore their ideas, wonder out loud, and make assertions is great learning—it is also a real energizer and helps them stay involved.

10. **Make notes to yourself.** You have probably already learned this by now, but it bears repeating: Keep copious notes about your training experiences with the clips. We are sure that, by referring to them sometime hence, you will find insights, places where you tripped up, and opportunities you can exploit the next time you use the clip. It is part of the responsibility you have of being a reflective trainer.

11. **Set up a computer file to make notes about movies.** Beyond the training experiences you will see in movies, you will also see scenes that you find informative, delightful, and fascinating. Because you now have a new way of looking at things, you will be able to see immediately the possibilities of using the scene in your work. Alternatively, you may experience another trainer using a clip that is applicable to your work. Or you may simply have a conversation with a friend about a movie or clip. Make notes on what the clip is about, who the characters are, approximately where it falls in the movie, and what is happening. At a time of your choosing, you can then add it to your collection by following the template we used in this book.

12. **Have fun.** The clips here and the ones we know you will develop on your own add immensely to the training experience. We are supposed to get involved with our emotions, our hopes and dreams, our wonderment, and our other senses. Too often our education and training are one dimensional and not nearly as stimulating as they could and should be. So, relax, have fun, and play together with these clips!

Index

**CORWIN
PRESS**

The Corwin Press logo—a raven striding across an open book—represents the union of courage and learning. Corwin Press is committed to improving education for all learners by publishing books and other professional development resources for those serving the field of PreK–12 education. By providing practical, hands-on materials, Corwin Press continues to carry out the promise of its motto: **"Helping Educators Do Their Work Better."**